GUERNSEY CONNECTIONS

Archaeological and Historical Papers in Honour of Bob Burns

Edited by Heather Sebire

First published 1998

ISBN 0 9518075 8 7

Cover illustrations

Front cover illustration: Pottery by Kenneth Barton

Back cover illustration: Sketch of Lukis Observatory by Anne Spencer

Published by

La Société Guernesiaise,
Candie Gardens,
St. Peter Port,
Guernsey GY1 1UG

CONTENTS

Bob Burns

FOREWORD

BY
PROFESSOR BARRY CUNLIFFE

This volume is a celebration of twenty years of intense and creative archaeological activity on the island of Guernsey. It presents a rich, eclectic, mix of papers embodying insight, wisdom and scholarship sharing in common an infectious enthusiasm for the subject. There could hardly be a more appropriate way of honouring Bob Burns. The various contributions of his many friends exactly reflect the man.

Bob came to Guernsey to live in 1962 and began excavating with Ken Barton at Château des Marais in 1975. From that auspicious beginning until his retirement in 1995 Bob worked tirelessly to advance our understanding of early Guernsey. These two decades have seen such a remarkable outpouring of new, and often surprising, information that we can fairly claim the archaeology of the island to have undergone a revolution.

Let us pause for a moment to consider what has been achieved. At Les Fouaillages entirely new light has been shed on Neolithic and Early Bronze Age burial ritual, while the remarkable trench through the defences of Jerbourg demonstrated for the first time that earthwork enclosures of considerable size were being constructed in the Early Bronze Age. Once begun they were maintained and enhanced over a long period, in the case of Jerbourg well into the Iron Age. The large-scale rescue excavation of King's Road provided an invaluable context for studying afresh and reassessing Guernsey's tradition of La Tène warrior burials. At the same time the excavation exposed a settlement dating to the early first century BC, when cross-Channel trade was intense, well into the second century AD. This was augmented by trial excavations at the rural settlement of Tranquesous offering an insight into the fascinating transition period from the Late Iron Age to the full Roman period. A few years later came the quite unexpected discovery of a Roman harbour-side settlement at La Plaiderie which must surely be the precursor of St. Peter Port. Nor was the medieval period neglected. The castles of Château des Marais and Castle Cornet were fully examined, work began at Lihou Priory, rural hamlets were discovered at Grandes Rocques and Albecq and every opportunity was taken to carry out rescue work in St. Peter Port. It has been a staggering achievement. In a brief span of twenty years Guernsey has been provided with a coherent and systematic archaeology covering six millennia. Against this, isolated discoveries made in the past can begin to be assessed anew.

The archaeological work inspired by Bob Burns on the island is of far more than local interest. It provides a vital link in our growing awareness of the intricate culture of the European Atlantic façade. At every stage in the story Guernsey has its part to play. It belongs to the European tradition and yet, by virtue of being a comparatively remote island, it has always retained a distinctive identity. Herein lies its continuing fascination.

In bringing together this series of papers under the title *Guernsey Connections*, written by Bob's friends and colleagues, the editor has chosen to reflect the island's position in the *longue durée* of the Atlantic tradition. It is a worthy tribute to a man whose tireless efforts have done so much to establish the basis for our new understanding.

Introduction

The reason for publishing this book is quite simple. It is a tribute to the work of Bob Burns, in the field of archaeology in Guernsey, from many of his friends and colleagues. It is particularly appropriate that it is being published by La Société Guernesiaise, as it was the organisation which supported Bob's work in the initial stages before he was employed at Guernsey Museum. La Société has continued to support archaeological work in the island and members of the section have excavated on all the recent excavations. It was during that extremely hot summer of 1976 when I first visited Guernsey on holiday, that I initially met Bob Burns. He, along with many other locals, was taking part in Ken Barton's excavation at Château des Marais. After this dig, with Ken Barton's encouragement, the Archaeology Section of La Société was reformed and Bob organised excavations around the town area including the site at the Bordage. Later, I visited the site at Le Tranquesous where Bob's new found enthusiasm for archaeology was further strengthened by the excitement of finding a site that opened up a new chapter in Guernsey archaeology by bringing us to the attention of colleagues in both France and mainland Britain. At the time Bob, who originally came from Uxbridge in North London, was working for British Airways. His family were also running a guest house in St Peter Port but Bob still found time to apply his voracious appetite for knowledge and his curiosity for all aspects of the human condition not only to acquiring a considerable knowledge about Guernsey's past but also about his particular interest in ceramics. When the post of Assistant Curator became vacant at Guernsey Museum in 1980 Bob was appointed and later the post developed into that of Archaeology Officer. So for the next sixteen years Bob dug, published and lectured not only in Guernsey but in the other Channel Islands, as well as Britain and France. He put Guernsey well and truly on the archaeological map of Europe and provided a baseline of material, dug under modern conditions, which will be a reference point for years to come. Bob has now retired to France where we all hope he will enjoy many years of 'La Bonne Vie' and will spare a thought now and then for those of us who are carrying on where he left off.

Acknowledgements

My grateful thanks to all the contributors to this volume not least for their papers but also for their patience and co-operation in bringing the volume to publication. My thanks also to those who responded but were unable to write for the book. Marion Archibald made a small donation in lieu of an article.

I am indebted to Griff Caldwell for reading the texts, organising the final proofs and making editorial contributions and to La Société Guernesiaise for publishing the book.

Thank you also to the unnamed volunteers both in the field and the workshop, without whom a great deal of this work would not have been achieved.

The photographs are from the collections of Guernsey Museum & Galleries.

Finally my thanks to Joan Bagley, Barry Wells and Perry's for the typesetting and layout.

Heather Sebire
Editor

'Guardians of the Past for the Future!'

A REVIEW OF ARCHAEOLOGICAL RESEARCH IN GUERNSEY

BY HEATHER SEBIRE

When I arrived in Guernsey in 1978, leaving a job in archaeology in England and my family in Northern Ireland (to marry into the line of 'homo guernesiensis!') I was very often asked the question, 'Well, there won't be much archaeology over there, will there?' I was soon to realise happily, how wrong my questioners were, for I quickly discovered that Guernsey had a long established tradition of archaeological research and I had arrived at a time when Bob Burns, who became a major contributor to that research, was just beginning to develop his interest in Guernsey's archaeology. Even with the help of a crystal ball, I think it would have been impossible to predict how the next fifteen years or so would enhance and enlarge our knowledge of Guernsey's past and what major discoveries would be made.

Introduction

It is not difficult to imagine that our ancestors in Guernsey and elsewhere must have revered their past in much the same way as we do today. It is quite probable that the dwellers of the Bronze Age village community in the lee of the burial mound at Les Fouaillages, would have held the monument, which would have dominated their immediate landscape, in awe and reverence. If only the stones could speak and give us some idea of what those people actually thought of the tomb, which even to them would have been of some antiquity. Similarly those seeking to defend the islands from the French, at the beginning of the fourteenth century reused the prehistoric ramparts at Jerbourg as part of their defences. Whether these people were aware or in awe of the earth movings of a different age we can only speculate.

Peter Heylyn, however, who travelled to France and the adjacent isles in 1626 and published the results of his trip in 1658, was not impressed by Guernsey's antiquities.

It was also the last part of my intention, to do something in the honour of the islands, by committing to memory their Antiquities, by reporting to posterity their Arts of Government, by representing, as in a tablet, the choicest of their beauties; and in a word, by reducing these and the Achievements of the people, as far as the light of Authors could direct me, into the body of an history. But when I had a little made myself acquainted with the place and the people, I found nothing in them which might put me to that trouble.(p.280)

Presumably this implies that people in Guernsey were not aware that antiquities from their ancestors did indeed survive until some time later.

A manuscript surviving in the British Museum records how Guernseyman Samuel Bonamy was aware of megalithic remains in 1749. This work is the subject of one of the papers in this book. Later, the first recorded, and published look at Guernsey's archaeological past was in 1811, when Joshua Gosselin wrote a paper for the journal Archaeologia (XVII, p 254), describing the discovery of the La Varde chambered tomb by the Guernsey militia on exercises on L'Ancresse Common. The soldiers thought that they had discovered an artificial cavern, out of which they removed pottery and bones. Accompanying Gosselin on his visit to the site was a young man who had been born in 1788 and who, we are told, went home that day with a human skull under his arm. The young man was Frederick Corbin Lukis, who became Guernsey's greatest antiquarian and was the founder of the Lukis Museum. The collections of this museum later became the nucleus of the present Guernsey Museum Collection. Gosselin also cites three other megaliths in his paper and thus began the 'modern' corpus of published material on the archaeology of Guernsey.

As a result of this brush with the past, at the age of twenty three, Lukis began a lifelong fascination with archaeology and the natural sciences. He was self-taught but against all odds he went on to discover, record and try to protect the remains of Guernsey's ancient traditions (not that far removed from what we are doing to this day). Although to present day archaeologists his methods may seem crude, we are blessed by the fact that he made meticulous notes and etchings and left superb water colour sketches which were painted by his youngest daughter Mary Anne. He also collected the artefacts from these investigations and in addition to the papers published nationally on Guernsey archaeology (see Bibliography), his greatest endeavour was an archive called the Collectanea Antiqua in which he recorded his excavations and their findings. This opus consists of six volumes, unfortunately still unpublished in any form other than the original, which are housed at Guernsey Museum along with a number of his letters, notebooks and diaries. This body of work, although amassed without the scientific basis that modern day studies would provide and albeit now only one aspect of local archaeology, still forms a basis for any serious study of Guernsey's prehistoric past.

Many members of Lukis' family followed in their father's footsteps, although the focus of their studies was more widespread. His eldest son, Frederick Collings Lukis, published a paper in Archaeologia in 1853 (Vol XXXV, p232), in which he attempted to summarise the megaliths in the Channel Islands and elsewhere in a paper entitled "Observations on the Celtic Megaliths". His second son John Walter Lukis contributed to Oliver's report on the megaliths (see below), but the main bulk of his work was in France, where he conducted many excavations in the Côtes-du-Nord and Finistére. His third son, Reverend William Collings Lukis, worked in England and was particularly interested in the construction of ancient monuments. His collection of stone implements and pottery was bought by the British Museum after his death. It is thanks to Lukis's youngest son, Captain Francis du Bois Lukis, however, that we owe the contents of his father's museum which was bequeathed on his death, in accordance with his wishes, to the States of Guernsey. The States purchased the house in La

Grange where the father and son had lived and which housed this collection from 1909 until 1938 when it was moved to St Barnabas Church. The various papers published by the family are listed in the bibliography, many of which refer to the Channel Islands and Guernsey in particular.

In 1869, it was again a military presence, this time in the form of Lieutenant S.P. Oliver, R.A. who added to the growing corpus of knowledge about Guernsey's past. He was invited by the Ethnological Society of London to prepare a report on the condition of the prehistoric monuments on Guernsey. He published two papers which list all the sites which were known at that time which include drawings and plans mostly from the pen of J.W.Lukis.

Frederick Corbin Lukis died in 1871 leaving a wonderful legacy for present day researchers. It was not until some years later however, in 1890, that a new society, The Guernsey Society of Natural Science and Local Research (which had been formed in 1882 under the title of the Guernsey Science Society), began to publish annual reports of its Proceedings. The society had extended its name to take account of the growing interest in 'archaeology, folklore and language of the islands of the Bailiwick'. It would be tempting to write at this point the immortal phrase 'and the rest is history,' but in fact, it is only by listing the archaeological achievements as reflected in the Transactions of the newly named 'La Société Guernesiaise' that the story unfolds.

First half of the 20th Century

The records in the early 1900s list various finds of prehistoric pottery, flint and bone from sites that are now well documented, e.g. Le Crocq and Fort Richmond in St. Saviour.

The transactions of 1910 detail the first discovery at the Palaeolithic Cave site of La Cotte de St Brelade in Jersey and there was great speculation at the time as to whether a similiar site would be discovered in Guernsey. We now know from marine and palaeoenvironmental studies that this is unlikely, although not impossible due to changes in sea levels and the different periods of detachment from the mainland of France (Renouf and Urry 1976).

In 1912 Colonel de Guérin carried out an excavation for La Société on the site of megalithic cists-in -circles at L'Islet. A delightful contemporary photograph records a visit to the site by members of La Société Guernesiaise. The excavation did not produce any human remains, but pottery was recovered, including a complete vessel with small perforated lugs. The site was consequently left half exposed and protected by a fence, forming an early example of monument preservation in Guernsey! In 1914 a possible neolithic potters kiln at Noirmont, St Sampsons, was recorded prior to its destruction due to quarrying. The following year Colonel de Guérin and A.Collenette carried out a small excavation at Le Déhus monument but it was later in 1918 that the exciting discovery of the carving on one of the capstones was made, still one of the very few pieces of megalithic art in the island. This was followed in 1921 by the publishing of a list of dolmens, cists and menhirs compiled by Col. de Guérin. A much greater number were recorded then than sadly exist to-day but this is a valuable reference for present day scholars. In 1923 the Transactions record that the earthworks at Jerbourg were examined after a furze fire on the St Peter Port side and a map of the area was drawn up.

In 1928 a milestone in Guernsey archaeology was reached when T.D. Kendrick M.A. from the Department of British and Medieval Antiquities at the British Museum was invited by Dr R.R.Marett of Jersey to write a book in two volumes on the Archaeology of the Channel Islands, Volume One of which was on the Bailiwick of Guernsey. In the preface, Kendrick belittles his work as merely ' a thin and reluctant trickle of information'. How ironic that this is still revered as a standard work. In desciding the work of previous generations Dr Ian Kinnes of the British Museum descibes the work thus: 'The major if derivative treatments of Kendrick (1928) and Hawkes (1939) stand effectively alone' (Kinnes 1988). The Hawkes reference is to Volume Two, The Archaeology of Jersey. In the Guernsey volume Kendrick draws heavily on the Lukis material but the result is a scholarly and readable tome which is still a useful reference work today.Two years later in 1930 an excavation took place at Le Déhus dolmen supervised by Miss Collum for the States of Guernsey, the results of which are published in the Transactions of 1932. Some repair work was carried out at this time on the interior of the tomb and on the outside encircling wall. In 1938 the States purchased the island of Herm and work was carried out there to clear and identify the monuments.

The war years brought research to a halt and of course left an indelible scar on the landscape. It is difficult for us examining the landscape today to imagine it without the German defences. Of course these have already become an historical aspect of the island, but ravaging many earlier sites in the process.

The immediate post-war years

In 1952 a historian, Professor J. Le Patourel and his wife carried out an excavation at Lihou Priory, which was the first in a series of pieces of work which they undertook on Guernsey. Professor Le Patourel also worked on medieval documents relating to Guernsey and the other Channel Islands which are of enormous benefit as a basis for future work.

The Prehistoric Society visited the island in 1957. The party included the then Dr Glyn Daniel, from England, Dr P. R. Giot ,from France, and Dr A.E. Mourant from Jersey. Dr Daniel apparently asked for a re-appraisal of the Déhus site, but unfortunately it has not been possible to do this to date. Some 26 years later in 1983 the island again played hosts to the Society for its annual Spring Conference.

The 1950's and early 1960's saw some spasmodic work being done, for example on the briquetage sites at Fort Richmond and Le Crocq. In 1968 Professor and Mrs Le Patourel returned to Guernsey to excavate a medieval house at Cobo. Unfortunately this site which has so far yielded some of the earliest medieval material on the island,was only recorded in a summary report in 1981 by Peter Girard. Two further small excavations took place, one at Château des Marais with the help of boys from Elizabeth College, and one at Castle Cornet by the archaeology group, before a watershed period was reached.

Bob Burns 1975-1995

In 1974 Ken Barton, then Director of Hampshire County Museums Service, who had been excavating at Gorey Castle in Jersey, was invited by the States of Guernsey Ancient Monuments Committee, through the museum curator Rona Cole, to excavate at Château des Marais (or Ivy Castle). The site was run as a training excavation and as a result the archaeological excavation group of La Société was formed under the leadership of Bob Burns. It was thus that Bob's enthusiasm for archaeology was instilled and he became from that time on, until his retirement in July 1995, the driving force behind archaeology in Guernsey.The next twenty years cover a catalogue of work for which Bob Burns and the island can be justly proud.

In 1975 a briquetage site at Fort le Crocq was examined and the results published in the Transactions of La Société. The following year 1976, several sites in St Peter Port were excavated including one at the Bordage, St Peter Port. The subsequent report was the first published by Bob Burns. From this time on Bob's main interest was in medieval and post-medieval ceramics of North Western Europe.

The very hot summer of 1976 also produced some aerial photographs which were to lead to the discovery of a Late Iron Age settlement site at the Tranquesous, St Saviours. The photographs showed a ditch complex and hut circles and the subsequent excavation showed the first evidence for Iron Age settlement on the island which at the time was very exciting and was the first indication that Guernsey was on a major trading route in the Iron Age. In 1977 Professor Barry Cunliffe visited the site and pointed out the importance of these links in a public lecture entitled "Cross Channel Trade in the Pre-Roman Iron Age". He also wrote a preface to the excavation report which was published the following year:

The excavation at the Tranquesous marks a turning point in the archaeology of Guernsey, for not only is it the first such work to be undertaken on a reasonable scale and to modern standards on the Island, but it is the first settlement site of any date to be adequately explored by archaeological methods.

He goes on to place the Tranquesous in its European setting. This was also the beginning of Professor Cunliffe's active involvment in Guernsey and Channel Island archaeology, which has been of great benefit ever since, particularly with regard to the Iron Age. He summed up by saying, 'This is an important beginning to a new era in Guernsey archaeology. But there is much to be done.' Despite all that has been done these words seem to ring true some twenty years later. There still seems much to be done, but now it is to take forward the work of the last twenty years and ask more precise questions. This luxury would of course not have been possible without the corpus of work achieved by Bob Burns.

The medieval period was not forgotten, however, as also in 1977, a seond season of work took place at Château des Marais again directed by Ken Barton. This work was the beginning of Ken Barton's work on Guernsey castles which will shortly culminate in the publication of his work at Castle Cornet. The results of the Château des Marais excavations were published in the Transactions of La Société for 1980. Also at this time the site of briquetage working at Richmond headland was re-examined by the newly formed Archaeological Research Group of La Société.

A discovery that was to exhaust many superlatives was made in 1978 by two members of the archaeology group at Les Fouaillages at L'Ancresse. They had located what they believed to be a hitherto unrecorded megalithic chambered tomb. After preliminary investigations, Dr Ian Kinnes of the British Museum was invited to visit the site and he decided that the mound did indeed warrant further investigation. This was made possible by the Ancient Monuments Committee supporting Dr Kinnes in three seasons of work, starting in 1979, on what turned out to be an amazingly complex funerary monument of immense importance, which Dr Kinnes describes in his article in this book. In 1983 he published along with Jenny Grant a reappraisal of the other megaliths in the island along with the preliminary results from Les Fouaillages (Les Fouaillages and the Megalithic Monuments of Guernsey see Bibliography).

This period from the late 1970s to the early 1980s was a particularly busy time. In the summer of 1978 Ken Barton carried out an evaluation excavation on the site of Lihou Priory on Lihou Island off the west coast of Guernsey. This was followed in 1979 by the final season of work at the Château des Marais and in 1980 by an excavation at the Vale Castle. The ceramic evidence from these sites is discussed in Ken Barton's article in this book. Alongside these 'set piece excavations' carried out by visiting archaeologists, a great deal of work was carried on locally. In 1978 Bob Burns initiated an excavation at Jerbourg, St Martin's which ran for several years. This was originally thought to be the site of an Iron Age hill fort but in fact was revealed to be a multi period site from the late Bronze Age to the medieval period.

In April 1980 further developments in Guernsey Iron Age studies were made. Due to the vigilance of a local builder we were asked to look at a site in King's Road, St Peter Port which was later revealed to be a complex settlement of the La Tène period with a later Gallo-Roman phase. It is difficult now to describe how exciting these initial discoveries were, especially in the light of the Gallo-Roman finds that were yet to be made. But to have confirmation that this site proved the existence of early trade routes through the discovery of ceramics and other objects such as shale, again by Barry Cunliffe of the Institute of Archaeology in Oxford, brought other work into focus. The presence of the sherds of a complete Samian bowl on the King's Road site was a clue to the amount of Gallo- Roman material that was yet to come to light.

As so much new work was being undertaken, Peter Johnston, who was then Secretary of La Société Guernesiaise, invited speakers to a Symposium on Channel Islands Archaeology, entitled the International Conference on the Archaeology of the Channel Islands and Related Areas of Southern Britain and Western France . Experts from Britain, France and the Channel Islands themselves, read papers to the symposium and much vital new information was aired and exchanged. The results of this work were published in 1986 in 'The Archaeology of the Channel Islands' edited by Peter Johnston, (see Bibliography).

Meanwhile the digging continued. In 1982 a series of excavations began at Castle Cornet directed by Ken Barton for the States of Guernsey Ancient Monuments Committee. These excavations were to run for almost ten years and the results have been quite amazing. Not only has the evidence from the excavations challenged the long held belief about the dates for the first castle, but it has also provided a wealth of material which superbly illustrates the 'castle story' and has helped to provide a ceramic sequence for Guernsey, as Ken Barton discusses in his article in this book. The eagerly awaited forthcoming publication of the excavations at Castle Cornet will be a major reference point for medieval and post-medieval work in the future.In 1982, Mike Hill carried out a rescue excavation at La Hougue Catelain on L'Ancresse Common in the Vale parish. A small area of occupation survived despite quarrying and other activities in the area but the soft soils were being eroded by people walking over the site and the elements were also causing erosion. A good deal of decorated Bronze Age pottery was recovered but it was difficult to put it into context as so little of the site remained in situ. As further work on this period is done a sequence for the pottery may become easier to establish. The results of Mike Hill's work are published in the Transactions of La Société for 1990.

While such matters were going on in the terrestrial zone there was equal excitement about matters maritime. A local diver, Richard Keen, was out looking for scallops on Christmas morning in 1982 when instead he found a Gallo-Roman trading vessel sitting on the harbour floor. Richard Keen had already been in contact with Margaret Rule and so he asked her advice and as a result the Guernsey Maritime Trust was set up to record and excavate the wreck, which became known as Asterix. This work took several seasons of diving and eventually the wreck was raised from the sea bed in 1985. The wreck site report was published by Dr Jason Monaghan and Margaret Rule in 1990 in a volume entitled ' A Gallo-Roman trading vessel from Guernsey',which also listed other known wreck sites from St Peter Port harbour. In 1991 Dr Monaghan published a gazeteer of sites and pottery from St Peter Port harbour.

Meanwhile, back on dry land, in 1983 the Directors of Elizabeth College who owned the site at King's Road gave permission for a short excavation during the summer vacation. This excavation confirmed the importance of the

Major Archaeological Sites in Guernsey

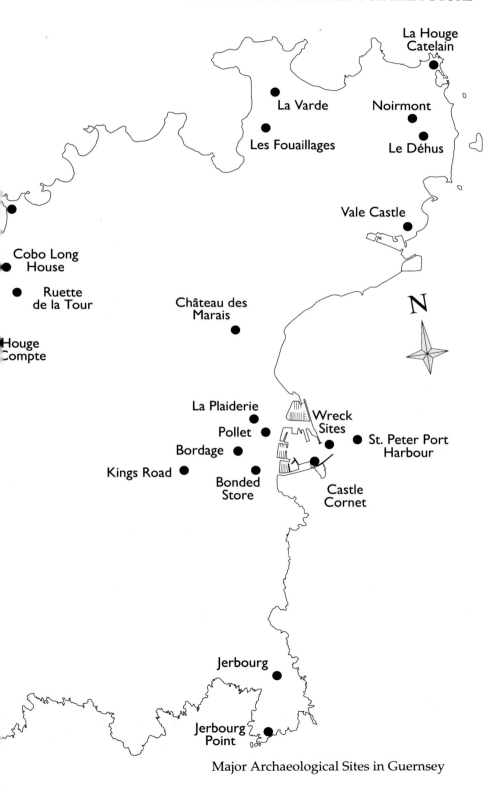

La Houge Catelain

La Varde

Noirmont

Les Fouaillages

Le Déhus

Vale Castle

Cobo Long House

Ruette de la Tour

Château des Marais

Houge Compte

N

La Plaiderie

Wreck Sites

Pollet

St. Peter Port Harbour

Bordage

Kings Road

Bonded Store

Castle Cornet

Jerbourg

Jerbourg Point

Major Archaeological Sites in Guernsey

site and gave a fuller picture of the two phases of occupation. At the same time, access was gained to an area of gardens slighty further to the south, in which area a cemetery site, contemporary with the first phase of occupation of the settlement (i.e. late La Tène) was discovered. Four graves were excavated, one of which was the grave of a warrior, complete with his accoutrements. Once again we were greatly assisted by Professor Barry Cunliffe in this work. This excavation also helped to enthuse a new generation of local students to study many aspects of local archaeology, one of whom, Philip de Jersey, completed a doctoral thesis on Celtic Coinage and has also written a paper in this book. There are so many areas that are yet to be examined in such detail that one can only hope that many more will study archaeology to this standard, which greatly helps to increase our knowledge in general. Another local student at this time, Mark Wood, began a detailed study of the ceramics of the Channel Islands and neighbouring France in the Late Iron Age and Gallo-Roman period. A third local student, Helen Nilen, studied the prehistoric period, again in the whole of the Channel Islands.

But there was more excitement to come. For generations Guernsey school children had been told that the Romans had never come to Guernsey. Evidence was building that this era had been misinterpreted due to lack of evidence. In 1985 Bob Burns began an excavation at La Plaiderie, in the heart of St Peter Port, which revealed the remains of two substantial Roman buildings suggested to be warehouses along the Roman waterfront. For the first time stratified Roman pottery and tile were found along with some interesting fine items, including a bronze cauldron foot, coins and part of a clay figurine. The stone drain belonging to La Plaiderie, the medieval court house of the town, was also located. The finds from La Plaiderie and the Gallo-Roman trading vessel are now superbly displayed in the Maritime Museum at Castle Cornet. In 1986 several sites that were being affected by coastal erosion were giving cause for concern and so an excavation was started at Grandes Rocques, Câtel on what was revealed to be an early medieval village settlement. Two apsidal buildings were found similiar in shape to buildings found on early medieval sites in Brittany which are the subject of Michael Batt's article in this book. 1987 saw the continuation of work at Castle Cornet, particularly at the Sutler's House, which yielded an amazing array of domestic artefacts from the sixteenth century.

Throughout the time from the late 1970's to 1988 local archaeology was greatly enhanced by the photography of Bill Tipping who in all weathers had made a photographic record of all the work that was carried out. Bill Tipping left the island in 1988 to live in Australia but made sure that his photographs were passed to the museum before he went. In 1990 Bob Burns directed an excavation at Lihou Priory which is situated on a tidal islet off the west coast of Guernsey. As mentioned above Ken Barton had carried out a small excavation in 1978 on the east end of the church, but the 1990 dig concentrated on the domestic buildings to the west of the Priory itself. The excavation was carried out with the help of the organisation Earthwatch who provided volunteers from the USA. Unfortunately the work planned for 1991 was cancelled due to the Gulf War and lack of funds.The following year in 1991, a new maritime museum opened at Castle Cornet, which included a great deal of information about the Gallo-Roman wreck and also about the excavations at La Plaiderie, which Bob was instrumental in putting together in his role as Archaeological Officer at Guernsey Museum. In 1992 a small excavation was mounted at Coupée Lane in St Peter Port which produced a great deal of post-medieval material and also showed evidence of clay extraction.

Bob Burns was called in as consultant archaeologist to assist the States of Alderney in 1992 to deal with an Elizabethan ship wreck which had been discovered off Alderney's northern shores. The wreck is recognised as being of international importance and although a considerable amount of preliminary work has been done the project is seeking funds to carry the work forward. The Medieval Society held their annual conference in the islands during 1993 and attracted many visiting archaeologists. Also in 1993 an excavation was carried out at Rousse Tower, in advance of its refurbishment as part of the Fortress Guernsey project. This project has been undertaken by the States of Guernsey to upgrade the island's many fortified sites, from the Neolithic period to the Second World War. During the excavation the rampart and the surrounding ditch were sectioned and five gun platforms were revealed, which were made from imported Portland stone. However to the west of the tower a prehistoric horizon was also located, which produced Late Neolithic / Early Bronze Age material.

In advance of refurbishment being carried out on one of the gardens at Castle Cornet, a small excavation started in 1994. This was in the garden named after General Lambert, who was a Cromwellian General who was imprisoned in the castle at the end of the civil war. The results from this excavation will be included in the main Castle report. Later in the year a chance find by a vigilant digger driver during drain laying at L'Ancresse was reported to the Museum. This consisted of a group of bronze objects which have been dated as belonging to the early Iron Age.

Conclusion

It was in 1994 that changes began to occur in the pattern of research. In June 1994 the untimely death of the Guernsey Museum curator, Rona Cole, led to a change in the regime at Guernsey Museum. An excavation at Albecq on Guernsey's west coast was to be the last that Bob Burns directed, as he became acting Director of Museums. The excavation which was undertaken because of coastal erosion revealed the walls of three buildings dating to the late fourteenth century. These appear to be a small proportion of a settlement which stretches along the lower headland at Albecq. By this time Bob had decided to retire, which he did in June 1995, but not before he had set up a research programme on an amazing group of pottery which had been retrieved from the harbour by

Richard Keen. This work is being undertaken by Robert Thomson and Duncan Brown who have written separately in this volume.

And so a new generation of researchers begin hopefully to carry on the tradition that has been established so ably over the last twenty years or so. Archaeology has become so inter-disciplinary and multi-disciplinary that it cannot function in isolation. Projects will now need to be carefully designed so that we get maximum information with the resources available. Bob Burns has illustrated what he and others before him have achieved. I look forward to bringing all this work together in the future to make sure that Guernsey's Past is recorded for posterity in the most up to date way possible. We are in the computer age (which will eventually have an interesting typology) but without the work of Bob and his predecessors there would be no base line to work from. I offer him this volume as a tribute and assure him that the work will go on.

Towards a Ceramic Sequence in Guernsey

BY

KENNETH J. BARTON

The archaeology of Guernsey has been the subject of interest for some 150 years principally in two phases, that of the Lukis family and their associates and after a long gap the revival of interest which was fostered by the late Rona Cole. In both these phases the Island was shown to have archaeological treasures above and beyond those which one might expect from a small island located off the coast of a continent.

The first phase of these activities was concerned with the megaliths and the contents of those burial chambers. These works and the resulting finds have been studied with an almost ruthless intensity in the past and in recent times by students reading for degrees in prehistory. But the contents of the megaliths have not contained ceramics of sufficient quantity to warrant the production of a definitive corpus so that we are lacking in our knowledge of the early forms of vessels. Field work in the Island has produced items of some importance such as at the Neolithic site at L'Erée. However we await the results of the excavations at Les Fouaillages to set us on the right road in placing the pottery discovered there in its proper context. That said, we are then left with the whole of the Bronze Age to be studied and the pottery to be put in sequence. At this point both in the archaeological context and in the history of Island archaeology there is a noticeable gap. From the Iron Age onwards we are fortunate that the material from these and all subsequent periods has been (more or less) covered; Bob Burns has had a hand in all of this.

His contribution to this rapidly widening range of artefacts has been to bring about the recognition that Guernsey is a place where archaeology is taken seriously rather than being one where only antiquarian interests prevail. He has seriously sought after the full range of this material and has never hesitated to obtain the very best advice in its identification. He has been faced with a series of rescue projects which have ranged in date from the Iron Age to the early 19th century. Most of this work, with some notable exceptions, has of necessity been undertaken against the clock but none the less under his direction a sequence of ceramic development has been established. This has been enhanced by the production of stratified groups found in excavations undertaken by him and others.

The Iron Age finds at the Tranquesous in St Saviour may have been small in number but they were the first of that era to be excavated. They were enhanced by the spectacular finds at the two-period Kings Road site, where the Iron Age site had itself been reoccupied in the second century A.D. The range of ceramics from this site gave a great insight into the place of Guernsey in the late Iron Age to Gallo-Roman cross channel trade.

The discovery, at last, of the Gallo-Romans in the island was quickly followed by the finds from La Plaiderie in St. Peter Port where four centuries of occupation were laid bare. This added to the sequence of imports of pottery from both southern England and the continent both near and far. Certainly after the beginning of the Gallo-Roman period all the pottery used in the island appears to have been imported and remained that way until the production of ceramic building materials at the end of the 17th century.

At this point one should mention the other side of the import business, that is pottery recovered from the harbour of St. Peter Port. Some wrecks, most notably a Gallo-Roman vessel, have been found and also the wood work of several other vessels, one of which at least is thought to be medieval. Although the ceramic collection from the harbour is quite diverse and of great interest for its own sake it does not greatly add to the sequence of socially used material. For instance the only Merovingian pottery so far recognised on the island is represented by two pots partially filled with tar which were probably lost during a caulking exercise on one or more vessels in the harbour. These do however point to ships and trade in that period. The pottery awaits discovery on inland sites. The work of harbour recovery undertaken by Richard Keen, a local diver and archaeologist, has been well supported by Bob Burns who has arranged for the study and subsequent publication of this fine group of material. The Guernsey Nautical Archaeological team has also contributed to the discovery of archaeological finds which has added to our knowledge of trade, direct or passing.

There is however a lack of material to fill in the years immediately after the Romans left. For example, on the nearby Cotentin Peninsular there are pagan Saxon burials and also Cherbourg was fortified to become one of the 'Saxon Shore Forts'. At the same time we know of the uninterrupted life of that city through the sixth century and onwards with the construction of a substantial church in the seventh century. However it would appear that the Channel Islands were in some disarray. The same is true of our knowledge of the ceramic sequence at least until the ninth century, by which time we are in the era of 'Normandy Gritty Ware', that ubiquitous and long-lived ceramic fabric that is common to all the centuries up to the 15th. The earliest examples of this ware come from two sites, the 'Long House', Cobo, excavated by Jean le Patourel and the 'Grandes Rocques' site directed by Bob Burns. The pottery from the 'Long House' may be as late as the end of the 11th century as the structure was dated by association with a carved bone roundel of early medieval design. The pottery from Grandes Rocques has within its group examples of early glazed wares which should put the date at least as far back as the ninth century. It is only these additional pieces that help to make the difference in dating, as specific identification of 'Normandy Gritty Ware' in fragments is very difficult.

The next in sequence and the first securely stratified group is that derived from the excavations at the Château des Marais. It was at this site that Bob Burns began his archaeological career. This site was shown to be a major work of construction and of two principal periods, the first of which was Medieval. This period was also divided into two phases, although these carried the date right through the 13th and into the early 14th century. The ceramic sequence at this site comprised in the first phase of 'Normandy Gritty Ware' and only a few fragments of glazed ware were found; one of these was thought to be English in origin. These wares date from early to mid 13th century. In the second phase there is again a domination by 'Normandy Gritty Ware' although there is a marked number of fragments of South Western French origin. There are also a significant number of English wares in this group, all of them readily paralleled at Southampton. The dating of the second phase ware is put to the end of the 13th century and into the 14th century.

This group of wares marks the first important change in the sequence of ceramic importation, although the phrase 'importation' is perhaps incorrect where the wares are not only common to Guernsey but also to the nearby Manche in Normandy. This is the common pottery of the area of which the Channel Islands is a part. The change is indicated by the out-of-area wares that begin to appear at this time. English pottery occurs as it does in other like sites after this date but never, until the 17th century, in any appreciable quantity.

The influx of Saintonge wares is significant. Although widely exported into the active ports of the British Isles and found in St. Malo, along the South Coast of Brittany and doubtless elsewhere on the French littoral, this is a genuine export that marks the change in trade as well as the change in Guernsey's relations with both England and France. A dump of this highly decorated Saintonge polychrome ware has been found in the harbour of St Peter Port. It is also present in the levels marking the initial construction of Castle Cornet. Also at Castle Cornet we see running with and beyond the currency of Saintonge wares, the final phase of Rouen decorated wares which are usually small versions of the large strip decorated jugs but with small tripod feet. They take us through the 14th century when, towards its end, the pottery changes which sweep through the whole of Western Europe show their effect here.

The basic pottery form in use during the 14th century is still 'Normandy Gritty Ware' but towards the end of that century into the 15th it changes to its terminal form still in the same fabric but markedly coarser in quality. These vessels are decorated with an application of a red ochreous wash, roughly applied, principally to the area around the shoulder of the vessel. Over this, again very roughly applied, are splashes of a very dull green glaze which also occurs on various parts of the body. The pots, including their decoration and glazing, show a marked lack of finesse, a sad end to a type with a long and honourable period of servitude. Associated with this ware is another type unique to the sequence so far discovered. This is a ware called, for want of a better description, 'Chocolate Brown Ware'. As its name indicates it is similar in colour and texture to hard brown chocolate. This ware has been fired in a reducing atmosphere to a high temperature. It does have some quartz and other mineral inclusions as a natural part of its makeup. These two wares are always found in association with one another.

First recognised in Guernsey at the Vale Castle site, these wares have been found tightly grouped at Bob Burns's excavations at Lihou Priory in a guardrobe of the second phase of building. However of greater significance is the fact that these wares were found in a building at Albecq in association with a small hoard of coins which confirm the long held but previously speculative date of early to mid 15th century. At this time we also see the beginnings of the influx of Normandy stoneware.

This hard coarse purple pottery is still in production today and commonly offered for sale. Its development appears to have come out of 'Normandy Gritty Ware' for the early examples, which are found in kilns in and around Domfront, Normandy are very coarse in texture. It was soon refined and became the ceramic currency of the whole of the region in every direction. Furthermore its centres of manufacture also became widespread and by the 18th century there were at least three potteries in Le Manche, with well-documented export routes carrying on to the middle of the 20th century. The range of wares is considerable from the largest and coarsest of storage and manufacturing vessels to many and various items of general domestic use. It includes table ware, ornaments and building materials of which ridge tiles were widely produced and exported.

This ware dominates the 16th century although there is a widening of the imported items, which are reflected by the deposits of South Western French pottery together with the commonly found German stonewares. In the 17th century we see another momentous change in the importation of pottery from a different source, that is the products from the South East Dorset potteries located around Verwood. This ware becomes so common that it matches Normandy stone-ware in quantity and in any group those two will comprise 80% of all finds.

That state of affairs continued until the beginning of the 18th century when the military commenced the construction of a barracks at Castle Cornet, the building of Fort George and the refortification of the Château des Marais and the Vale Castle bringing new life and fresh vigour into the Island. With its trade routes guaranteed, Guernsey again became prosperous and therefore Verwood pottery and Normandy stoneware were relegated downstairs and the best of English, German, French and Chinese wares came into prominence. As Bob Burns showed in his rescue dig at the Guilles-Allès library, the quality of wares in common use in this small island was equal to, if not more varied than, that of any large English trading city.

In this piece I have tried to show the principal groups and the main markers in the ceramic progression. There is also a wide variety of other wares, the most noticeable of which are Spanish wares of all kinds and quality which occur in every level of every period in small amounts, marking a steady trade with the whole of the Iberian peninsular. Noticeable also is the comparative lack of English wares. We do not find the quantities of fine, early post medieval glazed wares which occur in Jersey. The sequence is revealed and set down and will become a useful aid to those who follow, thanks to the work of Bob Burns and others who have realised the need to establish reference material of this, the archaeologist's most enduring and reliable dating source.

This is the Place where Time Meets Space

BY

IAN KINNES

'....where nothing has any meaning,..... neither time nor space, and where what other men call success can no longer serve as a criterion.' (Josef Goebbels)

It would seem to be wholly inappropriate to begin with two Fascist-derived quotations (the title is from Parsifal) for a volume devoted to the Channel Islands and dedicated to Bob Burns. I shall, however, seek to justify it. This is avowedly a narrative account and falls broadly into two parts. It concerns the excavation of Les Fouaillages on Guernsey: how it was excavated and viewed at the time, and what it now, after the event, seems to signify.

The excavation: how it was

In 1978 a gorse fire on the edge of the fifth green of the L'Ancresse common golf course revealed a mound with a projecting large slab. Limited investigation by the discoverers, John and Cherry Lihou, clearly demonstrated an earthen construction with built stone elements. Guernsey had then surviving components of some dozen megalithic or related monuments, all presumably of Neolithic date, with evidence derived from earlier records, including place-names, of as many as sixty more (Kinnes 1988). Virtually all had been excavated or recorded by the prolific Victorian family Lukis (Kendrick 1928) and little further work, notoriously apart from a bizarre exercise at Le Déhus (Collum 1933), had taken place in this century.

Bob Burns, a fully-fledged product of the Ken Barton school of archaeology, was then secretary of the thriving archaeology section of La Société Guernesiaise, doubling as a baggage-handler for British Airways in his spare time. In the traditional way, although the prehistoric archaeology of the islands is essentially that of the Armorican massif, advice was sought in the Anglophone sphere. Glyn Daniel, doyen des mégalithes, was approached and suggested my name. Never having been to the islands and then only loosely conversant with Kendrick's classic work, an invitation to view was readily accepted when expenses were mentioned. Bob will recall our shared memory of our first meeting at Guernsey airport.

An inspection of the trench left us in no doubt that the mound was artificial, of sandy earth with the top of a retaining wall visible. Within the mound was the edge of a large granite block lying horizontally, perhaps a capstone. A few scattered pieces of flint and stone had been found. Full excavation was decided, financed by the States of Guernsey Ancient Monuments Committee and making extensive use of Guernsey Museum resources. The digging force, with the exception of some mainland imports, was provided by members of La Société Guernesiaise in any number on any day or even any hour and of any age from sixteen to eighty-odd. Such variability posed interesting strategic problems throughout.

The expectation was of course for a standard island dolmen - say on the lines of Le Trépied - and, we hoped, with contents intact. The emerging reality could not have been more different. There were times when interpretation was changing daily, often, and sometimes embarrassingly, live to the Channel Television camera.

The initial strategy got one thing wrong and one, as it critically turned out, right. The limited trenches of the first season were rapidly abandoned for total area excavation as it became clear that plan was more important than section. From the outset it had been agreed, or at least enforced by me on reluctant site supervisors, that all finds would be plotted in three dimensions and a permanent metric string grid maintained. The value of this, when we had estimated that a productive mound might yield fifty-odd artefacts, was manifest as the finds total moved into the thousands.

Two aspects of the structure emerged at an early stage. To our great surprise the retaining walls defined a triangular or trapezoidal mound, the first such ground-plan in the islands. This was very definitely a different sort of monument. Apparent disappointment lay on top of the mound at the east end where a megalithic chamber might have been expected. All there was seemed to be a formless jumble of massive boulders and rabbits had been busy in the area. If there ever had been a chamber it lay in total ruin. The discovery of giant claw marks along one side of the mound and local confirmation that a massive steam-shovel had quarried the common for sand during the Occupation seemed the final nail in the coffin.

The site could not, however, just be abandoned and there were still rays of hope. A precarious viewing from the top of an improvised 10 metre-high tripod suddenly realised that the boulders actually did form a built setting enclosing an oval space and few had been displaced. Continuing excavation produced a rectangular structure within that space, defined by a low wall of small blocks and ending against the upper parts of still-visible paired tall slabs of the earlier structures. In the area, usually displaced by the rabbits, major finds began to appear and eventually a superb matched set of eight fine barbed-and-tanged arrowheads emerged. A burial place or a shrine of the final Neolithic? There is no answer - any bones would not survive on such an acid soil and phosphate sampling proved to be a waste of time. The structure could not be readily matched elsewhere and its location on the crest of an existing mound and equipped, as it emerged, with a circular skirt of large boulders was a real novelty.

Reluctantly the structure had to be demolished because we needed to know about the mound beneath. The task was not easy. Fate was tempted by hiring the massive crane - some boulders weighed nearly a ton - for April 1st and Bob and I, the only two allowed by the insurers to work in the trench for this exercise, still have less than fond memories of accomplishing the feat in driving rain and near-glacial temperatures. Beneath the structure there was nothing but the neatly-stacked turves which formed the original mound. But there were finds and, here and there, in great profusion. It became clear that at intervals across and through the mound what can only have been separate basket loads of flintwork and broken pottery had been dumped, perhaps debris from a village midden.

The first assumption was, however, different. The decorated pottery was distinctive; in mainland France it could be dated to the earlier Neolithic and at least a thousand years before any other evidence for the first farmers in Guernsey. It could also be matched from pre-war excavations on the extraordinary site of Le Pinacle on Jersey. Jersey however was and is different. Until about 6,000 years ago it was still accessible by a dryland - or at least low tide - route from the Cotentin (fig.1). Farmers could, as elsewhere in Europe, have brought their herds and seed-corn on the walk. Guernsey, long isolated, needed boats for access, a new component of how the west was won (Kinnes 1984).

The answer seemed easy, for the site if not for the greater context. The pottery could not date the mound; we knew then in 1980 that mounds were Middle Neolithic. Early Neolithic was fortuitously preserved by a later cover. Settlement then monument; the sequence was easy. This was again wrong and revealed very dramatically. In the latter part of March 1981, towards the start of the third and final campaign, with little more than 89 centimetres of mound height to go, the Guernsey Evening Press ran the front-page headline 'Where is the chamber?' With only 75 centimetres of mound height left there could not be one, and I confirmed this to Channel Television, adding that perhaps it might have been in long-perished timber for which we had looked and failed to find. The following day came the capstone; there was the chamber, later to be demonstrated by the site dog, Muffin, as of dog-kennel size. At the same time, behind this chamber another rectangular stone-setting might have held burials also but here was the big surprise - a complete decorated pot had been placed at its rear, and the pot was early Neolithic - but monuments weren't built then. Radiocarbon dates were to confirm that they were, and for a while we had the earliest funerary monument in Europe; but why on Guernsey?

There was more to come: these structures were not the first on the site. The sequence began with a small trapezoidal cairn and terminal menhir covering a boulder-built cist with capstone and a nearby stone-paved hearth (fig.2). There were a few Early Neolithic sherds associated. These were covered by the trapezoidal turf mound defined at either side by boulder kerbs and at the east by a straight slab facade. At the centre of this a gap had been left for access to the first chamber, simply a rectangular space defined by turf walls integral to the mound. It may have been timber-roofed. This was remodelled: at the front the small chamber was inserted and at the rear two large upright slabs formed the back of the other chamber framed by low slabs. At its east end, which was open, was a pair of postholes. The space between the two chambers was infilled with dark earth, often burnt and rich in sherds and flints. Ultimately these went out of use, but not by casual abandonment. The rear chamber was carefully infilled with layers of small blocks and slabs, the front one with clean beach sand. The eastern entrance was blocked by a large slab completing the unbroken line of the facade.

Nothing happened for some two thousand years. Then, at the end of the Neolithic period, came the boulder structure on the top of the mound with its arrowhead deposit and, perhaps, burial. The defined space had been left open but built against the old kerbs and facade and abutting the circle was a broad skirt of massive blocks and boulders, the largest weighing over half a ton. Finally, the central space was infilled with earth. This was not all. A speculative trench in the flat area to the south of the mound, intended to establish whether flanking ditches were present, revealed something quite different. Here was a dense concentration of pits, postholes and a hearth, associated with material again of the final Neolithic. We cannot of course prove the strict contemporaneity of settlement and adjacent ritual structure but archaeologically they are of the same period.

Again we have a gap of two millennia or so and the site assumed a new character. The ancient mound formed the focus of a ditched field system, by its few finds of the late Iron Age and Gallo-Roman period. A ditch ran along the outside of the northern kerb and the kerb was extended to the west by the addition of further boulders. This extension was at first thought to be part of the original Neolithic structure but analysis in the protracted period of post-excavation work has shown otherwise. The ditch then turned at right angles along the eastern end of the mound, continuing south beyond the limits of the trench. This was presumably an arable system since clear evidence for shallow plough disturbance had been found in the settlement area. Intensive cultivation may have accelerated the deterioration of a thin fragile soil. The ditch fills gave clear evidence of repeated cleaning-out after sand blows.

This too was abandoned. A massive sand blow, perhaps more than one, covered the entire area, creating dunes in some parts. Gorse and bracken took over; the site was totally lost to view. Since then the common has served as pasture, as sand quarry here and there, as recreation for walkers, golfers, and archaeologists. The mound with its phase 3 chambers has been sensitively restored under the guidance of Bob Burns.

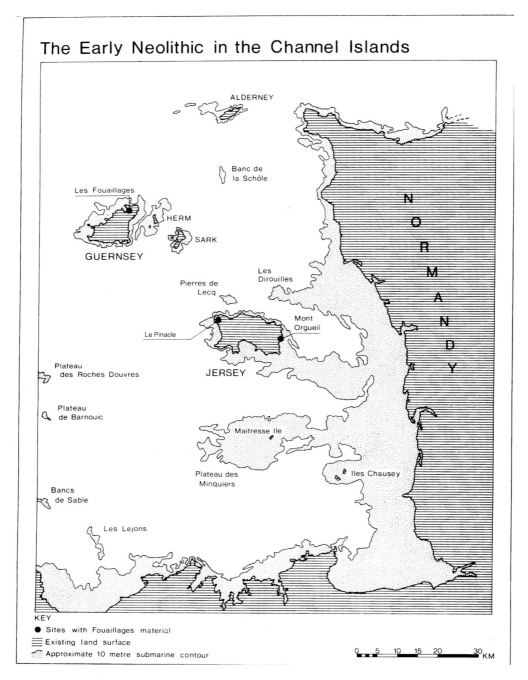

The Early Neolithic in the Channel Islands

KEY
● Sites with Fouaillages material
≡ Existing land surface
~ Approximate 10 metre submarine contour

0 5 10 15 20 30 KM

Figure 1.   The coastline of the massif Armoricain and adjacent islands in the 5th
millennium BC, with the distribution of earlier Neolithic sites in the islands.

The site: what it now means

In outline, therefore, the sequence and associations of Les Fouaillages were extraordinary. Archaeologists, and especially prehistorians, are fond of superlatives: earliest (sometimes latest), largest (rarely smallest), rarest (ideally unique), most elaborate (never simple), and so on. This leads to an element of distrust in discourse (for once an understatement). Apart from a naturally trusting local constituency who had to accept a gospel mediated by the site director whose words were sanctioned by the background presence of both the University of Cambridge and the British Museum, the world of prehistorians had to be convinced that this parade of novelties was plausible, persuasive and proven. We should list these novelties. They comprised earlier Neolithic (1-5) and final Neolithic (6,7):

1 The first sea-borne manifestation of the Bandkeramik tradition;
2 At the time, the earliest long barrow in Europe;
3 Both in structural form and in sequence, new types of chambers;
4 The practice of deliberate incorporation of midden material in the act of mound-building;
5 An intact decorated vessel of this period placed in a chamber? with the dead;
6 A new form of monument, apparently of funerary purpose;
7 A monument built deliberately on top of another and re-using some of its features.

This was a sizable agenda and one much rehearsed in many lectures, conference venues and some publications. Naturally, few in the Anglophone sphere knew enough of French and island prehistory to criticise. In France, it was harder but ultimately more successful work, accepted (by most) into the agreed data-base for subsequent interpretation.

So, to take this point by point:

The sea-borne Bandkeramik tradition

We immediately strike to the heart of a major and growing debate whose literature has become almost unmanageable. The crux of the matter is whether the cultivated crops and domestic animals which allowed and created 'civilisation' were brought to Western Europe by colonists from the east, driving the last hunter-gatherers before them; or whether the process was much more subtle, whether knowledge rather than people spread (some basic references and extensive bibliographies: Bailey ed. 1983, Bonsall ed. 1989; Clark 1980; Higgs ed. 1972, Hodder 1990, Price 1987; Reed ed. 1977; Whittle 1985, Zvelebil ed. 1986; Zvelebil 1994). I favour the latter view in modified form and for Guernsey see the knowledge of agriculture and the animals and seeds transmitted via an existing deep-water network of experienced fishermen (Kinnes 1982, 1984, 1986, 1988). Space here does not allow of further discussion of the intricacies of this debate.

The ancestry of the long barrow

At the time of excavation as what passed for, and therefore is, the real story emerged, comparanda were few. One could of course, point to the broad north and west European family of long barrows of the fourth and third millennia BC, so the general idea was there (Piggott 1966). Nearer to home the granite massif of the Cotentin, the closest mainland, had (and still has) nothing of help, either by way of structures or material. Brittany, however, did; over the previous century a kerbed trapezoidal mound style had been excavated and defined, notably by Le Rouzic in the Carnac area (summarised in Giot et al. 1979). This Manio type, often with multiple cists and often with 'ceremonial' objects in rare stones (jadeite, nephrite, callais etc.), was of uncertain date and estimates varied from early to late in the Neolithic.

The primary cairn, its menhir and the subsequent trapezoidal mound were well-matched by the Manio series. Also, a curious feature of construction lies in a deliberate asymmetry of the facade and the south kerb which were notably better built of more carefully selected slabs and blocks than the other side. This lateral distinction can be matched at certain Manio monuments (Giot et al. 1979). One might speculate whether turf-built chambers might have been missed by earlier excavators. The stone exotica were missing at Les Fouaillages but we did have the decorated pottery, then allied to the northern French Bandkeramik-derived Cerny group, and many associated fragments of schist bracelets.

Things have changed. Successively in the Paris Basin from the Yonne westward to just beyond the Orne cemeteries of massive long ditched enclosures, perhaps low mounds originally, have been identified and are linked to Cerny ceramics. This Passy-Rots style varies in ground-plan from cigar-shaped to trapezoidal and, like Les Fouaillages, has mortuary structures in the form of large wood or stone-lined graves with single burials set along the axial line (Duhamel & Prestreau 1991; inf. Desloges). We thus have a contemporary tradition with both structural and ceramic affinities with Les Fouaillages. More recently detailed analysis of the Western French evidence now convincingly places the Manio form at the head of the monumental sequence (Boujot & Cassen 1992, 1993; Kinnes & Hibbs 1989). Equally the association with the early Neolithic Castellic ceramics and re-assessment of the Pinacle-Fouaillages style suggests that both northern French and Breton influences created the insular tradition (Constantin 1985; Cassen 1993).

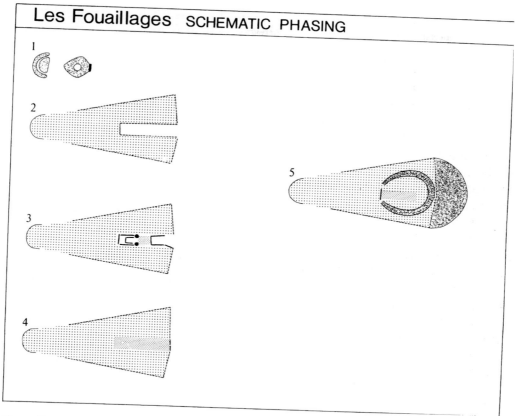

Figure 2.   A schematic sequence for the structures at Les Fouaillages.

New types of chambers

The turf-walled chamber continues to lack parallels for its structural method; as I speculated above such may have been missed in earlier excavations. It is, however, a perfectly acceptable precursor for the great range of non-megalithic structures which characterised the middle Neolithic floruit of long barrows (Kinnes 1992).

The dog-kennel chamber is easy to match in form, if not in size, but not certainly at this period. The western unroofed chamber with massive rear marker-slabs, subdivision and 'entrance' posts remains unmatched. The linear arrangement certainly recalls Passy-Rots practice.

Incorporated rubbish

Many monuments have yielded sparse scattered material from mound construction, none in the quantity of Les Fouaillages. It was thought originally that the material had, as elsewhere, arrived incorporated in turves cut from an overgrown former settlement site. The location of discrete dumps and not more or less continuous spreads denied this and this was further reinforced by the realisation that the structural asymmetry was also reflected in the relative quality of pottery and flintwork at either side of the axial. Before deposition, in other words, the 'midden' material has been sorted.

In an earlier context some source might be found for this practice. Some graves in Bandkeramik cemeteries seem to have been infilled with domestic debris rather than simple backfill. Equally the flanking hollows, originally borrow-pits, of Bandkeramik longhouses are often rich in material, commonly interpreted as rubbish thrown out of the house. It could equally be argued that, although no longer strictly functional, such material might be regarded as placed deposits referring back to the cognition of the original and its place within social perception.

Since a plausible argument can be made for the inspiration of the long barrow from the ancestral longhouse (Kinnes 1981; Hodder 1990) placed deposits, if such they are, provide added authenticity. Even more, a random piece of vandalism embellished this. After extensive rescue excavation in the Aisne valley had established intensive Bandkeramik occupation (Ilott et al. 1986), a replica longhouse was built for experiment, for visitors and ultimately and sadly for mindless vandals. The destruction by fire was however instructive (inf. Ilott). The sheer weight of timber and thatch in such a house burnt only slowly and some not at all. Some time after the event the house appeared as a low rectangular/ trapezoidal mound, its flanking ditches still perfectly apparent. If there is an element of fakery in long barrows, that is that they are meant to look ancestral, meant to look as if we have all been here some time, even in newly-won territory or new socioeconomic orientation, then such provides the model. This is what I think was happening in the volatile and precocious stages of what we now classify as the early Neolithic - monuments establish both place and the right to that place by appealing to tradition (invented) or the ancestors (largely legendary); (Hobsbawm & Ranger eds. 1983).

Grave-goods?

The intact, or rather crushed in situ, decorated vessel in the west chamber was certainly integral to the structure and its function. For the period, intact vessels are normally with single inhumations in flat graves in northern France. At more or less the same time, however, the Passy-Rots enclosures were appearing with the single grave now entering the monumental sphere. It may be reasonably safe to assume that Les Fouaillages is an allied but stone version. Recently the long mound at Erdeven, Morbihan, currently under excavation, has produced an axial unroofed cist with a rich inventory of stone ornaments and a complete decorated vessel of Castellic style (inf. Cassens). Here, again, acidic soil conditions prevented bone survival.

A new form of monument

There are no good parallels for this form of ring-cairn with central rectangular setting. The closest analogies must be sought in the cist-in-circle series in the Channel Islands where boulder rings enclose often massive cists, as nearby at L'Islet. Some seem to have had mounds, perhaps as a secondary feature. The idea of a central open space, later to be infilled, can be plausibly traced back to the passage grave tradition as illustrated on Jersey by Mont de la Ville and La Pouquelaye de Faldouet (Kinnes 1988).

Monumental succession

Re-use of chambers and burials inserted into the mound are of course common throughout western Europe. I know of no instance where a monument sui generis has been built on top of an existing structure. Successive additions to enlarge or extend mounds are again quite common but these are simply continuations of the original principle. Whether the long mound was still recognised for what it was two thousand years later is a moot point but the re-use of the still-visible paired stones as a focus of the new structure suggests that some recognition of symbol or status was attached.

Why Guernsey?

We should return to the original precepts of this paper. As figure 3 demonstrates the Channel Islands lie at a crossroads. Eastward is the Bankeramik tradition with longhouses and, finally, long mounds. Southward is the Atlantic seaboard with long mounds, passage graves and Castellic pottery, perhaps ultimately influenced by the Mediterranean Impressed Ware tradition. The Pinacle-Fouaillages style is a distinctive insular variation blending characteristics of both the epi-Bandkeramik Cerny and the Breton Castellic. The role of marine communications has been much underestimated and we can be reasonably sure that as the elements of the new Neolithic economy and technology spread westward, there was already in place an effective and knowledgeable marine network. For its early date and its location this really is the place where time met space.

The Goebbels quotation was chosen as a deliberate contrast. This vision of the ultimate totalitarian state has no room for the discovery which changes perceptions. As Les Fouaillages revealed itself to us and then to a wider world we confirmed yet again that intellectual freedom and sheer curiosity are a vital part of being human. I have tried to tell a plain unvarnished story. It cannot convey the intensity and range of memories associated with the excavation and its extraordinary and talented team, but most particularly with the collaboration and friendship of Bob Burns.

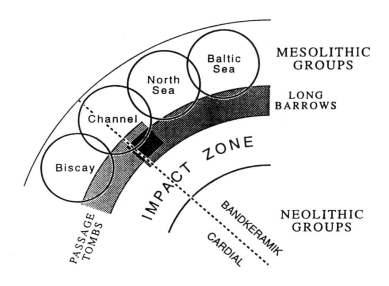

Figure 3.   A temporo-spatial model for the neolithisation of north-west Europe.

Bibliography

Bailey, G. (ed.) 1983 *Hunter Gatherer Economy in Prehistory*, Cambridge.

Bonsall,C. (ed.) 1989 *The Mesolithic in Europe*, Edinburgh.

Boujot, C. & Cassen, S. 1994 Le développement des premières architectures funéraires monumentales en France occidentale, Colloque Interrégionale sur le Néolithique, Vannes, *Revue Archéologique de l'Ouest* Sup. 5, pp195-211.

Boujot, C. & Cassen, S. 1993 A pattern of evolution for the Neolithic funerary structures of the west of France, *Antiquity* 67, pp479-91.

Cassen, S. 1993 Material culture and chronology of the Middle Neolithic of western France, *Oxford Journ.Arch.* 12, pp197-208.

Clark, J.G.D. 1980 *Mesolithic Prelude*, Edinburgh.

Collum, V. 1933 The Re-Excavation of the Déhus Chambered Mound at Paradis, Vale, Guernsey, *Transactions La Société Guernesiaise.* Vol XII p7

Constantin, C. 1985 Fin du Rubané, Céramique du Limbourg et Post-Rubané: le Néolithique le Plus Ancien en Bassin Parisien et en Haunaut, *BAR S273*, Oxford.

Duhamel, P. & Prestreau, M. 1991 La Nécropole monumentale néolithique du Passy dans le contexte du gigantisme-funéraire européen, in J. Despriée et al (eds.) *La Region Centre: Carrefour d'Influences?* Argenton-sur-Creuse.

Giot, P-R. et al. 1979 *Préhistoire de la Bretagne*, Rennes.

Higgs, E.S. (ed.) 1972 *Papers in Economic Prehistory*, Cambridge.

Hobsbawm, E. & Ranger, E. (eds.) 1983 *The Invention of Tradition*, Cambridge.

Ilett, M. et al. 1986 Douze années de sauvetage dans la Vallée de l'Aisne, in J.P. Demoule & J. Guilaine (eds.): *Le Néolithique de la France*, Paris.

Kendrick, T.D. 1928 *The Archaeology of the Channel Islands Vol 1: The Bailiwick of Guernsey*, London.

Kinnes, I. 1981 Dialogues with death, in R. Chapman et al.(eds.): *The Archaeology of Death*, Cambridge.

Kinnes, I. 1982 Les Fouaillages and megalithic origins, *Antiquity* 56, pp24-30.

Kinnes, I. 1984 Microlithis and megaliths: monumental origins on the Atlantic fringe, in G. Burenhult: *The Archaeology of Carrowmore*, Stockholm.

Kinnes, I. 1986 Le Néolithisation des Iles Anglo-Normandes, *Actes du Xe Colloque Interregionale sur le Néolithique*, Caen.

Kinnes, I. 1988 The Cattleship Potemkin: reflections on the initial Neolithic in Britain, in J. Barrett & I. Kinnes (eds.): *The Archaeology of Context*, Sheffield.

Kinnes, I. 1992 *Non-Megalithic Long Barrows and Allied Structures in the British Neolithic*, B.M. OP 52, London.

Kinnes, I. & Hibbs, J. Le Gardien du Tombeau: further reflections on the initial Neolithic, *Oxford Journ. Arch.* 8, pp59- 66.

Piggott, S. 1966 Unchambered long barrows in Neolithic Britain, *Palaeohistoria* 12, pp381-93.

Price, T. D. 1987 The Mesolithic of Western Europe, *Journ. World Prehistory I*, pp25-305.

Reed, C. (ed.) 1977 *Origins of Agriculture*, The Hague.

Whittle, A. 1985 *Neolithic Europe; A Survey*, Cambridge.

Zvelebil, M. (ed.) 1984 *Hunters in Transition*, Cambridge.

Zvelebil, M. 1994 Plant use in the Mesolithic and its role in the transition to farming, *Proc. Prehist. Soc.* 60, pp35-74.

The Preservation of Megalithic Monuments in Georgian Guernsey

BY

RICHARD HOCART

The surviving megalithic monuments of Guernsey are a fraction of those which once existed. In an article published seventy-five years ago T. W. M. de Guérin identified a number of otherwise unrecorded monuments from land records dating back to the fourteenth century.[1] These monuments had already been destroyed when Joshua Gosselin and Frederick Corbin Lukis carried out the first surveys of the island's antiquities. Lukis and Edgar MacCulloch recorded the destruction of several more monuments in the nineteenth century: La Gibet des Faies at L'Ancresse and the large passage grave known as La Rocque qui Sonne were broken up for building stone at the beginning of the century, followed later by the grave called La Creux des Fées at Les Paysans, the menhir of La Rocque Pointue and Le Tombeau du Grand Sarrazin.[2]

Scholarly interest in antiquities grew in Britain during the eighteenth century, and in Guernsey the earliest known initiative to preserve a megalithic monument was taken before the middle of the century by a leading native of the island. He was Samuel Bonamy (1708 - 1770), who became Bailiff of Guernsey in 1758. In 1749 Bonamy wrote *A Short Account of the Island of Guernsey*. This unpublished manuscript is now in the British Museum. Bonamy gives a short description of the megalithic monuments as this extract shows:

"The first religion practised in the island was paganism. For it appears that the ancient inhabitants were pagans by their altars; three of which remain at this day, upon which they used to offer sacrifices to the gods of the sea. They consist of flat ragstone, of a vast bulk and weight, supported three or four feet above the ground by three or four lesser stones, on which they are so artfully laid, that they seem hardly to touch them, and where they do touch, the diameter is scarce two inches wide; and yet, which is very surprising, they have remained in that position above seven hundred years. Of the three which are yet left in Guernsey, two are in the Vale and one in St. Saviour's parish. This last was being destroyed by the owner of the ground, to prevent which I purchased the land. … After our dukes had given encouragement and protection to people to remain in these islands, the Christian religion soon expelled the mists of paganism and in time they built churches as likewise monasteries and other religious houses."[3]

At the end of his manuscript Bonamy drew a small map of Guernsey on which three pagan altars are marked. One is clearly Le Déhus, another is probably La Platte Mare, both in the Vale, and the third is the passage grave at Le Catioroc in St Saviour, which Bonamy labels as 'a Pagan Altar (mine)'.

Bonamy was aware that some monuments had not survived. What is surprising is that he mentions only three surviving monuments. The folklore attached to some other monuments, such as the passage grave at Le Creux ès Faies at L'Erée, which is still well preserved today, strongly suggests that they were known in Bonamy's time to the inhabitants of the districts in which they lie. Bonamy's interest was in structures which were recognisable as altars, and while he may have been aware of others such as Le Creux ès Faies, he evidently saw no cultural association between them and his 'altars'. Over sixty years later, when knowledge of antiquities had made some progress, Gosselin recorded only the same three 'temples' and the recently discovered monument at La Varde in the letter describing the island's antiquities which he sent to Sir Joseph Banks in 1811.[4]

After Bonamy's intervention to save the passage grave at Le Catioroc, the next recorded act of preservation was the purchase of the passage grave at Le Déhus by John de Havilland in 1775. According to Lukis, de Havilland intervened at the last minute to save the monument from destruction for building stone.[5]

The third monument to be preserved on the initiative of leading island citizens was the passage grave at La Varde. According to Kendrick, Lukis dated the original discovery to 1793 or 1794, when some soldiers of the Duke of Mortemart's regiment discovered the capstones.[6] In fact this French emigré regiment was in Guernsey from February to November, 1796, and Lukis seems to have placed the discovery two or three years too early.[7] A partial excavation was carried out by the soldiers, after which the monument was abandoned and it filled up with wind-blown sand.

A second excavation took place in the summer of 1811. It was carried out by soldiers of the garrison and Kendrick suggests that the initiative for the excavation may have come from Sir John Doyle, the Lieutenant-Governor. In his letter to Banks, Gosselin concluded his account of the excavation with the remark: "As this temple stands upon the top of a hill it is the intention of some gentlemen in the island to have so much of the sand on each side of it removed as may render it visible to all the surrounding country".[8]

New information about the gentlemen to whom Gosselin was referring has come to light in the papers of Peter de Havilland, the Bailiff of Guernsey at the time, who was, incidentally, the brother of John de Havilland. On 24 February 1813 and again on 7 May de Havilland wrote to his great-nephew, Thomas Dobrée at his home in Nantes. De Havilland informed him that the 'Druids' Temple' excavated in 1811 stood on land which had belonged to Dobrée's grandfather, Thomas Dobrée (1728-98), who had sold the land but had reserved the rights to all the stone. Dobrée junior, as one of his grandfather's heirs was part-owner of the monument, and, as he was unable to attend to his affairs in Guernsey owing to the war between France and Great Britain, de Havilland was acting as his attorney. De Havilland said that he had visited the site during excavation and that it was proposed to enclose it with a wall.

Dobrée's reply does not survive among de Havilland's papers, but de Havilland's next letter to him, dated 7th May 1813, indicates that Dobrée was considering buying the site of the monument. De Havilland warned him that it would be necessary to protect the monument with a seven foot high wall:

"...pour garantir ce temple de la brutalité de nos paysans ...Tu sai qu'il faut à leur regard mettre zéro en ligne de compte du respect et de la vénération qu'on doit naturellement avoir pour les antiquités."[9]

No further correspondence on the matter is recorded, and it appears that Dobrée did not buy the monument. Furthermore, there appears to be no evidence that the wall was actually built, but photographs taken later in the nineteenth century show that the mound had been removed and the monument exposed rather in the manner envisaged by Gosselin.[10] Despite its exposure it remained untouched by the population of the neighbourhood.

The date when Dobrée senior sold the land around the monument has not yet been established, but his decision to retain ownership of the stones suggests that he was aware that they were an antiquity and that he was anxious to protect them.

Although the disappearance of many of Guernsey's megalithic monuments during the eighteenth and nineteenth centuries is a grievous catalogue of destruction, three of the finest monuments were saved by the initiative of individual Guernseymen long before the true age and function of these structures were understood.

Figure 1.

References

1. T. W. M. de Guérin. 'List of Dolmens, Menhirs and Sacred Rocks.' *Transactions La Société Guernesiaise*, Vol IX p 30.

2. T. D. Kendrick 1928. *The Archaeology of the Channel Islands, Vol.1, The Bailiwick of Guernsey*. London.

3. S. Bonamy. 'A Short Account of the Island of Guernsey.' Brit. Museum. Additional MSS 6253.

4. Part of Gosselin's letter is reproduced in E. MacCulloch 1903 , *Guernsey Folklore*. p 134.

5. V. C. C. Collum. 'The Re-excavation of the Déhus Chambered Mound.' *Transactions La Société Guernesiaise*. Vol XII p 7.

6. Kendrick. op cit. p 107.

7. C. Hettier 1885 . *Relations de la Normandie et de la Bretagne avec les Iles de la Manche pendant L'Emigration*. Appendix.

8. MacCulloch. op cit. p 135.

9. Documents in the possession of Mr. J. A. de Havilland.

10. See, for example, the photograph of 'Dolmen of La Varde before 1898' in *Transactions La Société Guernesiaise*, Vol IX p 468.

Celtic Coins in Guernsey

BY
PHILIP DE JERSEY

Perhaps the most significant of Bob Burns's many contributions to the archaeology of Guernsey is his important work on the Iron Age in the island, and in particular the excavations of the Tranquesous and King's Road. For the first time, these sites provided information on the island's Iron Age excavated to modern standards, which combined with the wealth of detail recorded principally by the Lukis family has immeasurably improved our understanding of this period. In this paper I would like to consider an aspect of the Iron Age which has so far almost wholly eluded excavators on Guernsey, either ancient or modern: Celtic coins. The first part consists of a catalogue and comments on the small collection of Celtic coins held in the Guernsey Museum, most of which were found outside the island. In the second part I will examine the evidence for discoveries of coins in the island, and consider briefly why they are still so rare.

Celtic coins in Guernsey Museum

The Guernsey Museum and Art Gallery holds fourteen Celtic coins, thirteen of which are attributable to the Armorican tribe of the Coriosolitae, who occupied the eastern part of the Côtes-d'Armor. The Coriosolitae struck a series of staters and quarter staters, divided into six classes (Colbert de Beaulieu 1973, pp107-117), in the years immediately preceding the Gallic War. These coins, particularly the three later classes (I-III), were produced in colossal numbers: more than 30,000 have been found in a series of hoards on Jersey and on neighbouring parts of the French mainland. The six classes are divided into two distinct groups, but the significance - spatial, temporal or otherwise - of the break between classes IV-VI, and I-III, is not yet certain (de Jersey 1994, pp98-99).

Eight of the Coriosolite coins were found in the La Marquanderie hoard, discovered on Jersey in 1935 (Rybot 1937). They are listed below with reference to the die varieties identified by Rybot (1952). All the coins are base silver staters (see figure 1).

1.	Class III	Rybot 75	weight 6.23 g.
2.	Class I	Rybot 18	weight 6.28 g.
3.	Class II	Rybot 32	weight 6.40 g.
4.	Class II	Rybot 32	weight 6.15 g.
5.	Class V	Rybot 60	weight 6.50 g.
6.	Class I	Rybot 18	weight 6.09 g.
7.	Class III	cf. Rybot 83	weight 6.33 g, reverse worn.
8.	Class V	Rybot 62	weight 6.62 g.

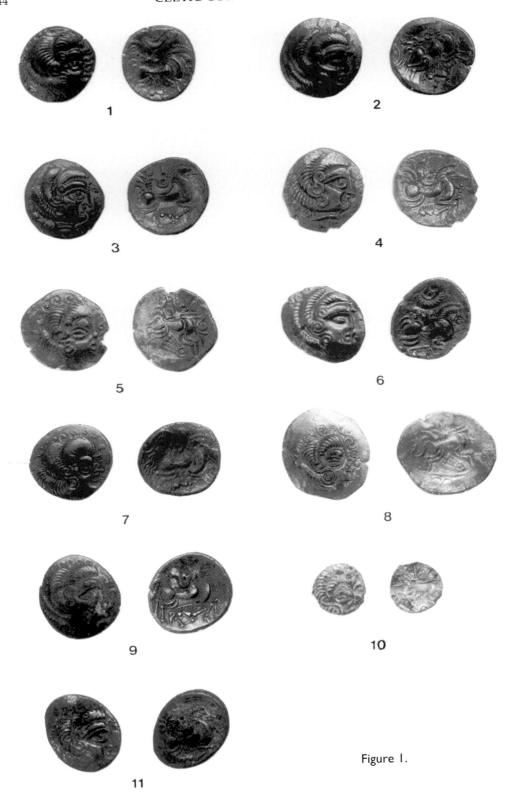

Figure I.

The La Marquanderie hoard forms probably the largest single deposit of coins ever discovered in the western Celtic world. Rybot estimated (1952, p12) that it contained almost 12,000 coins, all but a handful being staters of the Coriosolitae; more than three-quarters of these belonged to the three later classes of the series. Although most of the coins were donated to the Jersey Museum, a number were retained by private collectors or dispersed, including the eight now in the Guernsey Museum. As such a tiny proportion of the original find, probably chosen for their generally good condition, the Guernsey coins clearly have no great significance in relation to the original discovery.

A further three coins of the Coriosolitae in the Museum are believed to have been collected in Brittany by J. W. Lukis in the mid-nineteenth century. Their details are as follows:

9.	GMAG 5751.	Stater, class II, Rybot 32 .	weight 6.38g.
10.	GMAG 5752.	Quarter stater, class V. Small test-cut on reverse.	weight 1.46g.
11.	GMAG 5753 .	Stater, class II, Rybot 32 .	weight 6.61g.

Another three coins are on display in the Museum. Two are Coriosolite staters and one is unidentifiable:

12.   GML 1980/1. Class II. Found by a metal detector user at Richmond, Vazon, c. 1980. Weight not available.

13.   GML 1980/2. Class II. Found by a metal detector user at Richmond, Vazon, c. 1980. Weight not available.

14.   Unidentified stater. Said to have been found in Guernsey. Heavily corroded, weight not available.

Celtic coins found in Guernsey

A number of antiquarian writers of the early twentieth century refer to discoveries of Celtic coins in Guernsey, but it is almost impossible to establish the veracity of their reports. Most of them seem to be based on the collection of coins formed by Colonel T. W. M. de Guérin: thus Bourde de la Rogerie (1922, p114) notes that "Des monnaies gauloises ont été parfois trouvées a Guernesey", and illustrates six Coriosolite coins from the de Guérin medaillier, said to have been found in the island. The coins include two class III staters (probably Rybot 75 and 78), two class II staters (both Rybot 32) and two class V quarter staters.

De Guérin himself, in a slightly earlier paper on the Bronze and Iron Ages in Guernsey, makes no mention of his coins but comments that "In the Lukis Museum we have also seven Gaulish coins found in Guernsey of the type of the coinage of the Coriosolites... Ours consist of 5 staters and 2 quarter staters" (1918, 138-139). It seems unlikely that he would choose to ignore the provenance of coins in his own collection in a survey of Iron Age material found in the Bailiwick, if they could definitely be said to have come from Guernsey, and that reason alone should cast doubt on their origins. The possibility that they were found between his publication of 1918 and the 1922 article of Bourde de la Rogerie should also be considered, though had this been the case they would almost certainly have been recorded in the Transactions of La Société Guernesiaise.

The coins "found in Guernsey" in the Lukis collection are equally problematic, and it should be emphasized that no such finds are recorded in F. C. Lukis's *Collectanea Antiqua*. Nor do the more reliable historians of the nineteenth century, such as Duncan (1841) or Tupper (1876), mention local finds, although the latter (1876, p9) refers to discoveries in Jersey and might be expected to record any in Guernsey had he known of them. It is a distinct possibility that one or more of the Jersey hoards provided the coins which were said to have come from Guernsey. Most of these hoards were rapidly dispersed to an assortment of museums and private collectors, with little record made of this process.

Later writers are no more precise on the subject. Curtis (1935, p257) states that "Up to the present not more than 20 Gaulish coins in all... have been recorded as having been found in Guernsey...", but again the basis for this claim is uncertain. Marshall-Fraser (1948, p302) simply combines and repeats earlier records, but wisely avoids mentioning a particular figure: "There have been small finds of Gaulish coins, some of which passed into the collection of the late Col. T. W. de Guérin." It is undoubtedly significant that in the first authoritative survey of the island's archaeology, Kendrick (1928) does not mention any Celtic coins found in Guernsey.

For the first certain provenance of an Iron Age coin in Guernsey we have to wait until 1958, when a very small-scale excavation of a briquetage site at Le Catioroc produced a bronze coin (Jee 1958). This coin was sent to the British Museum, where it was identified by Derek Allen as the bronze core of a gold-plated stater of the Aulerci Cenomani. From the photograph of the heavily corroded coin which accompanies Jee's article it is impossible to confirm this attribution, but Allen's competence as a numismatist is unquestioned and there is little reason to doubt his word. Coins of the Aulerci Cenomani are relatively rare beyond the confines of the modern department of the Sarthe (de Jersey 1994, p185), although three were found in the Le Catillon hoard on Jersey in 1957, and another stater less certainly of the Cenomani is recorded from the same island (McCammon 1984, p39; de Jersey 1994, p59). The Cenomani series may have been produced for some considerable time from the late second century BC, and thus without a clearer identification the dating of this particular example must remain uncertain.

In more recent years the two Coriosolite staters recorded above (nos. 12 and 13) provide the only certain additions to the list of Celtic coins from Guernsey. Thus 150 years or more of antiquarian and archaeological endeavour leaves us with a grand total of three coins, from two sites on the west coast of the island (figure 2). This is in startling contrast to the pattern of finds from Jersey or indeed the nearest parts of the French coast, where as previously indicated many thousands of coins - mostly of the Coriosolitae - have been recorded during the same period (figure 3). We therefore need to ask whether the observed discrepancy is significant and, if so, why is Guernsey so different?

In the first place, we can almost certainly rule out accidents of fieldwork or recording, both in the nineteenth century and more recently. Both islands have been intensively cultivated and intensively quarried, the two processes which gave rise to many of the antiquarian discoveries (Hibbs 1986). If hoards of coins similar to those from Jersey had been discovered during the last century in Guernsey, at the period when Lukis recorded a number of warrior burials found by quarrymen, we can be sure that they too would have been recorded, at least in passing. Similarly, discoveries in the century since the founding of La Société Guernesiaise would almost certainly have found their way into the archaeological reports in the Transactions, but - except for the Cenomani coin discussed above - they have not. While there is always the prospect of the unexpected discovery of a hoard breaking the rule, at present we can say with some confidence that the phenomenon of Celtic coin hoarding in the Channel Islands appears to be confined to Jersey. The burial of a hoard of phalarae and Gaulish (but not Armorican) silver coins, which was found in Sark in 1718 (Allen 1971), was certainly a significantly later and non-Celtic event; the exotic origin of the objects suggests deposition by a Roman soldier, or may even be indicative of Gallo-Roman occupation on Sark which has yet to be archaeologically identified.

The hoards found on Jersey and around the neighbouring Armorican coast have traditionally been interpreted as indicators of the unrest caused by Caesar's campaign of 56 BC. Thus the hoards in the Cotentin are seen as marking the northward flight of refugees from Viridovix's battle with the Roman forces, perhaps in the region of Le Petit Celland. Some of the hoards were undoubtedly deposited at this period, including perhaps the La Marquanderie find. But other hoards are certainly later: at least two of the hoards found at Rozel in Jersey contained Roman denarii, in one case down to 39 BC and in the other 32 BC (de Jersey 1994, 169-170). These hoards may be indicative of further episodes of rebellion or unrest in Armorican Gaul, events which are unremarked in classical literature and not yet identifiable in the archaeological record. Although containing no Roman coins, the hoard from Le Catillon in Jersey has also been dated to a similar period, perhaps between 40 and 20 BC (Fitzpatrick and Megaw 1987).

The obvious explanation for the presence of these coins in Jersey but not in Guernsey is the geographical proximity of Jersey to the French mainland: Jersey

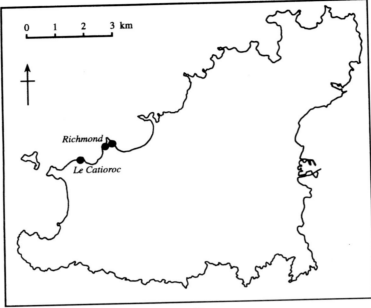

Figure 2. Confirmed finds of Celtic coins in Guernsey.

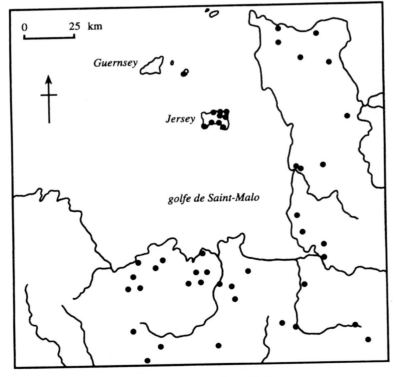

Figure 3. Celtic coin hoards from the Golfe de Saint-Malo
region (data from de Jersey 1994).

would be the natural first choice for refugees from disturbances in Armorica, whether at the time of the Gallic War or in the following decades. But there may be more complex factors behind this decision. There is no particular reason to assume that Jersey and Guernsey were under the same political control, and I would suggest that the archaeological evidence suggests just the opposite. Jersey may have been on friendlier terms with the Coriosolitae, while Guernsey may have had different loyalties reflecting its better position on the cross-Channel trade routes. On the basis of both recent excavations and antiquarian finds, Guernsey is considerably richer in fine late La Tène Armorican pottery, for example, and it may not be unreasonable to see a link between this relative wealth and the presence of numerous late Iron Age warrior burials on the island (Burns 1993). The lack of any such burials on Jersey is surely significant and, as with the presence or absence of coin hoards in the islands, is unlikely to be the product of differential rates of fieldwork or recording.

Guernsey undoubtedly holds several advantages over Jersey as a stop-ping-off point on the journey across the Channel, not least the existence of landing-places on the east coast, sheltered from the prevailing south-westerly winds. It would also seem to make more sense to stop at the last safe haven before the difficult stretch across the open Channel, rather than at Jersey. I have argued the case for the importance of Guernsey's role elsewhere (de Jersey 1993), but it remains difficult to identify who was trading through the island. Until relatively recently, Caesar had the defining word on this subject, writing in *De Bello Gallico* (III, 8) that "The Veneti exercise by far the most extensive authority over all the sea-coast in those districts, for they have numerous ships, in which it is their custom to sail to Britain..." Excavations at Alet, Saint-Malo (Langouet 1984) and Hengistbury Head (Cunliffe 1987) have to some extent shifted the balance in favour of Coriosolite control of the trade route, but there are several reasons to suggest that the importance of Alet - and hence of the Coriosolitae - has been overestimated. There are significant problems in accepting the chro-nology proposed by Langouet (de Jersey 1993), and the use of coinage as indicative of Coriosolite control may be misguided. There is little evidence that any Armorican coinage was struck primarily for use in external exchange, or indeed for everyday economic use within a tribe, and it is difficult not to associate the massive outpouring of coinage at the end of the Coriosolite series with the need to pay troops fighting Caesar. It remains the case that Celtic coinage is extraordinarily rare in stratified pre-conquest levels on Armorican sites (Gruel 1990), an absence which would seem to present the strongest evidence against its incorporation into normal processes of exchange. The Coriosolite coins at Alet (Colbert de Beaulieu 1974) are arguably from a post-conquest context (de Jersey 1993,p324), as are those in stratified levels at Hengistbury Head (Cunliffe 1987,pp136-140), where they may again reflect refugee movement rather than trading contact. If the role of the Coriosolitae and Alet in pre-conquest trade is regarded as relatively less important, we might expect to see the favoured trade route running round the Armorican coast rather than across the peninsula. Just such a route is suggested by the distribution of amphorae (Fitzpatrick 1985,p310), and it is conceivable that this route was controlled by the Veneti - just as Caesar wrote. Identifying the presence of the Veneti in this region - either in trade or in the movement of refugees after the War is, however, made particularly difficult by the lack of a coinage which can be unequivocally associated with them. Although there is a base silver coinage, similar in style to that of the Coriosolitae, which is traditionally attributed to the Veneti (Colbert de Beaulieu 1953), the distribution of that coinage (de Jersey 1994, 212-213) leaves considerable room for doubt on its origins. If the Veneti did control cross-Channel trade we should therefore not necessarily expect numismatic evidence for this role, on two counts: the absence of coinage from external trade at this period in Armorica, and possibly the absence of a significant Venetic coinage of the period anyway.

If Guernsey did hold a "pro-Venetic" position prior to the Gallic War, we should not therefore expect to find coinage on the island to confirm this. After the War, it presumably suffered from the defeat of the Veneti and a consequent diminution in cross-Channel trade, and as both more distant than Jersey and perhaps less receptive to the Coriosolitae, never experienced the arrival of the Armorican refugees who brought the hoards to the larger island in the succeeding two or three decades. This might appear to be a rather too convenient way of explaining the absence of coins on the island, and indeed there is a danger that we are ignoring the archaeological maxim "absence of evidence is not evidence of absence". But I would argue that the sum of antiquarian and archaeological research in the Channel Islands should by now be sufficient to confirm that the difference in the distribution of coinage between the two largest islands is genuine; it is simply unfortunate that the interpretation of this difference rests largely on negative, rather than positive evidence. It will be the task of Bob Burns's successors to provide this aspect of evidence for an Iron Age which has otherwise been so well served.

Acknowledgements

I am grateful to Peter Sarl, Heather Sebire and the staff at St John Street for allowing me to examine the coins in the Guernsey Museum collection. My greatest debt is of course to Bob Burns, for his many years of encouragement and support.

Bibliography

Allen, D. F. 1971: The Sark hoard. *Archaeologia* 103, pp1-31.

Bourde de la Rogerie, A. 1922: Les monnaies gauloises des Iles de la Manche. *Transactions of La Société Guernesiaise* Vol IX, pp111- 115.

Burns, R. B. 1993: Warrior burials in Guernsey. *In Les Celtes en Normandie* Revue Archéologique de l'Ouest suppl. 6, pp165-171.

Colbert de Beaulieu, J.-B. 1953: Une énigme de la numismatique armoricaine: les monnaies celtiques des Vénètes. I, le Billon. *Mémoires de la Société d'Histoire et d'Archéologie de Bretagne 33*, pp5-52.

Colbert de Beaulieu, J.-B. 1973: *Traité de numismatique celtique* 1. Méthodologie des ensembles Paris, Les Belles Lettres; Annales Littéraires de l'Université de Besançon 135.

Colbert de Beaulieu, J.-B. 1974: Les monnaies gauloises d'Alet. *Dossiers du Centre Régional Archéologique d 'Alet 2*, pp49-55.

Cunliffe, B. W. 1987: *Hengistbury Head, Dorset. 1: The prehistoric and Roman settlement, 3500 BC - AD 500* Oxford University Committee for Archaeology Monograph 13.

Curtis, S. C. 1935: Report of the Antiquarian section for 1935. *Transactions of La Société Guernesiaise* Vol XII, pp256-262.

De Guérin, T. W. M. 1918: Evidence of man in Guernsey during the bronze and early Iron Age. *Transactions of La Société Guernesiaise* Vol VIII, pp127-141.

De Jersey, P. E. 1993: The early chronology of Alet, and its implications for Hengistbury Head and cross-Channel trade in the late Iron Age. *Oxford Journal of Archaeology* 12, pp321 -335.

De Jersey, P. E. 1994: *Coinage in Iron Age Armorica* Oxford University Committee for Archaeology Monograph 39.

Duncan, J. 1841: *The History of Guernsey; with occasional notices of Jersey, Alderney, and Sark, and biographical sketches* London, Longman and Co.

Fitzpatrick, A. 1985: The distribution of Dressel 1 amphorae in north-west Europe. *Oxford Journal of Archaeology* 4, pp305-340.

Fitzpatrick, A. and Megaw, J. V. S. 1987: Further finds from the Le Câtillon hoard. *Proceedings of the Prehistoric Society* 53, pp433-444.

Gruel, K. 1990: Les monnaies gauloises en Armorique, présence ou absence dans l' habitat. In *Les Gaulois d 'Armorique* Revue Archéologique de l' Ouest suppl. 3, pp63-69.

Hibbs, J. L. 1986: Post depositional transforms and the megalithic distributions of the Channel Islands. In Johnston, P. (ed.) *The Archaeology of the Channel Islands* Chichester, Phillimore, pp207-224.

Jee, N. 1958: Archaeological report, 1958. *Transactions of La Société Guernesiaise* Vol XVI, p313.

Kendrick, T. D. 1928: *The Archaeology of the Channel Islands Vol 1. The Bailiwick of Guernsey* London, Methuen.

Langouet, L. 1984: Alet and cross-Channel trade. In Macready, S. and Thompson, F. H. (eds.) *Cross-Channel trade between Gaul and Britain in the pre-Roman Iron Age* Society of Antiquaries Occasional Paper New Series IV, pp67-77.

Langouet, L. 1987: *Les fouilles archéologiques de la zone des Cathédrales d'Alet* Saint-Malo Dossiers du Centre Régional Archéologique d'Alet suppl. L.

McCammon, A. L. T. 1984: *Currencies of the Anglo-Norman Isles* London, Spink.

Marshall-Fraser, W. 1948: The coinages of the Channel Islands. *Transactions of La Société Guernesiaise* Vol XIV, pp298-332.

Rybot, N. V. L. 1937: Armorican art. *Bulletin of Société Jersiaise* 13, pp153-190.

Rybot, N. V. L. 1952: Armorican art *Bulletin of Société Jersiaise*.

Tupper, F. B. 1876 (2nd ed.): *The history of Guernsey and its bailiwick: with occasional notices of Jersey* London, Simpkin Marshall & Co.

Armorican Inheritance up to the Iron Age

BY

PIERRE-ROLAND GIOT

Seen and dreamed about from over the water, the Channel Islands have appeared as a sort of 'Lost Paradise' for continental geologists and archaeologists, even if in recent times, as along most European coasts, excessive residential development may have spoilt or ruined parts of the scenery. Of course, up to a certain degree, this idealization was in common with most Atlantic islands, though those like Ushant, Molène, Sein, Groix, Belle-Ile, with more ferocious and wild shores, were different from the proximate ones, like Bréhat archipelago or the Ile-de-Batz, smaller rocky paradises. All of them were full of traditions, legends and even allusions in classic or Dark Age texts. This last source of information may have been lessened for the Channel Islands by their inclusion in the duchy of Normandy (though the life of Saint Maglorius gives some nice insights).

The 'miracle of conservation' (i.e. survival), as I call it, is the major factor in archaeological possibilities, most information having always been destroyed, and the representativity of what is left survives and leaves a crucial problem. The Channel Islands may have certainly been an archaeological paradise, although a strange one, reflecting the specificities of a particular series of landscapes.

Let us leave aside the different Palaeolithic Men. They profited from the solidity of high level natural caves in less weathered granite cliffs than those we have around the other coasts of the Armorican Massif, where we would relish to have them. Surface residual scatters of Mesolithic flints are everywhere equally miserable at a first glance. They have suffered from the same plague as the settlements of the Neolithic and Bronze ages, that is, the gradual soil erosion on the hills and slopes; all too rare are the sites where some evidence has survived because it was protected under some colluvium, some peaty marshland or some old sand dune. These last types of situations, being quite often around the level of the present tidal range, are too quickly eroded by the sea. Quite a few of such sites have gradually been observed in the Channel Islands, Normandy, Brittany, Poitou and elsewhere. They give an idea of all the intensively inhabited lowlands that have been lost around the coasts of the Armorican Massif. If one remembers the fantastic number of megalithic monuments once observed on the little islets of the Molène archipelago (nowadays largely destroyed because of the activities of sub-modern sea-weed collectors, hunters and others), a lost landscape or a smaller Scilly Islands configuration, also very attacked by the rough ocean surges and tidal currents, one can imagine all the settlements around those 'hills' that those islets must have been. Some relics have also been observable under the sand of beaches of the Léon and Trégor coasts, often on the border of present estuaries; small samples have been dredged from under sandbanks. Of course the land bridge between the Channel Islands and the Cotentin must have been such a favourable settlement zone (leaving aside the 'plank' of the Bishop of Coutances).

If the study of prehistory had been imagined by, let us say, Iron Age people, what a wealth of observations they would have been able to collect, as the sea-level may have had a stand-still or even a slight regression during this period. Quite possibly they did indeed, of course informally, and this could explain quite a lot of their curious activities around megalithic sites. The 'druids', or whatever their wise men were, have left us no memoirs of this! What a loss.

This does not imply that the more favourable hills of the interior were not inhabited during the Neolithic and Bronze ages; there is plenty of evidence for that. All the information from the interior of Brittany shows a diversified pattern. Neolithic and Bronze Age people were not only efficient herdsmen and gardeners (palynological evidence of serious clearing and crop-growing is chiefly only evident from the Bronze Age onwards), but also most capable rock and ore prospectors.

This experience and knowledge about very specific crystalline rocks and stones and ores was of course very effective for the production of tools and small objects, with techniques quite different from flint knapping (or quartz, quartzite and other replacement materials utilized in the Palaeolithic and Mesolithic periods with efficiency). The petrology of Neolithic stone axes and implements has led to much evidence about the specific sources for axes, pendants, beads and the like. There is however a chronological problem about which we cannot yet be over-confident; the impression is that the oldest axes in passage graves could be nice flint ones imported from outside the Armorican Massif, in the same way as the eclogite (and jadeite etc) symbolic axes have been imported from the Alps (in spite of very many Armorican sources of eclogite), the symbolic serpentine perforated discs also from the Alps and possibly the variscite (so-called Callaïs) beads from Spain. The local resources of fibrolite quickly procured a good substitute for many of these importations, as did other local minerals. Local epi-metamorphic schists were used for perforated discs in Central and Eastern Armorica and amphibolite and chlorite for those of the Western district (unhappily only finds of fragments with no chronological contexts); chronologically these discs could more or less correspond to the Pinacle in Jersey, a source of dolerite for perforated picks. The numerous Armorican sources of dolerites, metadolerites and amphibolites for stone axes have been rather put in the shade by the massive quarries of the Plussulien A metadolerite and their inflation of rough-outs and objects, diffused at a distance. Though this last material has been seldom utilized for prestige objects or symbols of power.

On the contrary, the small source of metahornblendite of Pleuven has only produced a limited series, chiefly perforated symbolic and prestige objects (110 only are known, including the broken ones and rough-outs), distributed over Northern France; the material, convenient for this type of working, would not be suitable for real tools. A very remarkable fact is that this material from Pleuven is the one utilized for the small sculpture, of the end of the Iron Age, of a musician (or god) playing a lyre, found thrown away after a mishap in a fire in a ditch of the large hill-fort of St Symphorien at Paule, Côtes-d'Armor. This is again a prestige or cult object. Three other metahornblendite statues have been found recently - but between the later Neolithic period (Chalcolithic) and this advanced Iron Age we know of no other objects made out of this remarkable ultrabasic stone. This is a reminder of expertise during the Bronze Age of Armorica for working most of the finest rocks which could easily have been found utilized for 'jewellery'; though a few 'status symbol' sticks were produced from diverse stones in the Early Bronze Age, as if the importation of some amber or jet was more rewarding.

The potters of the Armorican Massif have also worked on materials largely very different from those of the large post-Palaeozoïc sedimentary basins, such as the Paris, London or Hampshire basins, where only sedimented clays were used. Apart from very small Cenozoïc deposits, the Armorican potters utilized alteritic composite materials derived from the weathering and disaggregation of the crystalline eruptive or metamorphic bedrocks. From the Neolithic onwards, they, or at least some of them, thus acquired particular experience and expertise. This is especially true from the Iron Age onwards, where one discerns more distinct professionalism at the artisan level (though some Bell Beaker makers were most effective). As in the scope of stone objects, petro-archaeological studies have been very successful for the study of pots and potsherds, joining mineralogy, petrology and geochemistry techniques. This is especially true if one has good experience and knowledge of the field geology of the regions involved. It is not only a pure laboratory guessing machine. Practice in the field gives the knack.

Improving intuitive discoveries of some Neolithic and Bronze Age potters, and the Iron Age ones, especially those of the northern and western coasts of Armorica, have demonstrated the advantages of the clays and tempers deriving from the alteration of basic and ultrabasic (mafic and ultramafic) eruptive and metamorphic rocks, which are rather more frequent in those districts. The advantages can come either from the abundance of minerals with a structure in chains (such as amphiboles), giving coherence to the matrix, or from the abundance of certain phyllites (such as talc or chlorite) adding a certain resistance to thermal shocks and thermal loss.

These minerals, especially if in the temper one finds a chunk of rock with all its different minerals associated, give the archaeological detective nice clues to the origin and trade of certain fine or typical wares, more often at a medium distance (up to about 100 km), or by sea routes further away; pots being quite

'Breakables'. Apart from Mediterranean amphorae, and their probable use, again, the traffic of some pots opens a mystery question: were they traded empty, or was there some foodstuff inside? I have joked about the 'Coriosolite rillettes' sent to Hengistbury Head in the fine cordoned ware pots made with the Trégomar-Lamballe gabbro. Curiously, up to now as few sherds have been available for petro-archaeological studies, the Channel Islands appear, as far as pottery is concerned, rather confined to home-made products, which of course have benefited from the savoir-faire of the other Armorican potters.

Promontory sea-cliff forts are distributed all along the Atlantic façade of Western Europe, making use of natural features of the coasts. Traces of Neolithic occupation are widespread on them, though rarely relics of structures such as ramparts survive. Bronze Age habitation has often been overlooked; it has prepared the place for the Iron Age. These types of structures, though promoted by the cliffs of old rocks that are well consolidated, are not of course specific to any period.

Western Armorica offers at least three important categories of field monuments which can delimit its specificity: the Armorican Bronze Age barrows, the Armorican Iron Age stelae and the Armorican Iron Age souterrains (these last always associated with hill-forts or settlements). Their distribution corresponds, with some outlyers, to the territories of the Iron Age Osismi, western Coriosolitae and western Veneti tribes. Probably it is conservation problems which have blurred the extension to the eastern parts of the territories of the Coriosolitae and Veneti. One could possibly consider the Osismi, the Coriosolitae and the Veneti as the Super-Armoricans; the more eastern tribes being in a gradual transition to other zones of Gaul.

With less assurance, could one go backwards and consider, for instance, that the Late Neolithic female statue-menhirs, which are only known in Guernsey and on each side of the Laïta estuary (separating Finistére/Morbihan), on the southern coast of Brittany, were also a specific proto-Armorican invention? Or more generally that the know-how of the mastership of granite shown by the different successive generations of Armorican megalith-builders was the result of a regional tradition, as opposed to the work with tree-trunks or simple limestone rocks, so easier to deal with? This may be overdrawing the evidence.

If copper is scarce in the Armorican Massif at least at the surface level, as we cannot be interested in deep lodes associated with ultrabasites, iron is available everywhere under numerous mineral forms. Modest placers with gold are widespread. Gold-panning is simply a question of patience and spare time, with from time to time a nice nugget. Indeed, there are traces of working in the Iron Age on different sites. Lead lodes are very numerous in the Armorican Massif and galena is widespread, which includes silver of course. And there were plenty of cassiterite lodes and placers. The Iron Age extraction of salt from the sea is of course well known nowadays. Without having the potentialities of a rich production zone for metals or common substances of the mineral world, Armorica was fairly well off. Indeed, one is rather surprised by the comparatively modest booty from the Iron Age that has been retrieved. This may be the result of a tendency to scrounge and to recycle, also of alteration and rusting severely along the coasts. A lot of hoards may have been discovered during Medieval agricultural extensions, on account of the small depth of the soils and the continual erosion. Because of the strained relations between landowners and tenants, so many gold objects, coins or hoards have been dissimulated, sold to jewellers and melted down; those that went into a commercial circuit generally appeared at a great distance from the discovery spot, more often very imprecise.

After this very general overview, let us consider islands and small lands assimilable to islands. Those not very far from the mainland, all around Brittany, have been intensively frequented from the Mesolithic times onwards. With the Postglacial rising sea level, some, at the beginning easy to get at, may have had a temporary desertion until new sailing facilities were available: this would be the case of the 'drowned landscapes' around the Houat and Hoedic group of islands, or the Molène archipelago. The Quiberon peninsula is geomorphologically an island; we do not know exactly when the sand tombolo attaching it at present to the continent took place, or if there was a period, between the Bronze Age and the Iron Age for instance, when it was again an island at high tides. The sea did sometimes cut it, when storms and spring-tides coincided in the XVIIIth and XIXth centuries. In spite of this, there are plenty of Late Bronze Age and Iron Age remains. On the Channel coasts, the small islands and rocks in front of the Abers of North Finistère, the Ile-de-Batz, the Sept-Iles and the Bréhat archipelagos show plenty of evidence with specific cases. Groix has been less easy to get at, but large enough to be well populated. In a slightly different way, the coasts being low instead of high, the Glénan archipelago was probably another 'drowned landscape', though with less numerous traces of different occupations, which might express an episodical interest, through all periods.

Ile de Sein must have always been quite difficult to get at (except in very fine weather). With the Chaussée-de-Sein towards the west, there must have been an elongated 12 km 'drowned landscape', nice for coastal supplies. Though most have been destroyed since a century, there were traces of plenty of small megaliths on Sein. Pomponius Mela tells us about the priestesses of Sena insula, in front of the coast of the Osismii, a correct localization of an unverifiable legend, as if the last inhabitants after the rising sea level were these wild women, possibly not at all wild in reality. They may have been only ghostly apparitions of fishermen lost in the storms!

More comparable in size to the Channel Islands are Belle-Ile and Ushant (Ouessant), which according to recent studies, begins to be better appreciated than it was. Mesolithic people may have still been able to come there dry-shod. There were Neolithic inhabitants, having perhaps some peculiar funeral traditions, owing to the relative isolation introduced by the arrival of the sea. Better equipped, the Iron Age ones developed promontory forts, though other types of sites of that period are lacking, perhaps because of local conditions not showing them up. On the whole, Belle-Ile does not appear as a very distinct centre of activity.

This contrasts with the results of recent discoveries and excavations at Ushant, *Uxisama*. There major occupation seems to begin with the Neolithic period; no Mesolithic people could have arrived without a boat. This is proof that Neolithic men did largely practise seafaring, at least in fine weather, in dangerous regions. Because the island has not been intensively cultivated in post-medieval times, and more browsed by sheep, the surprise has been a large settlement at Mez-Notariou, excavated since 1988 onwards, with thousands of post-holes, hundreds of houses, a sort of town-planning with rows and roads, diverse traces of metal-working, all this in two principle groups, one from the Late Early/Middle Bronze Age, the other from the First Iron Age, with traces of later occupations. What did such an organized village do on a wild island at the extreme western part of this section of Europe? Even for food, it would have had to rely largely on what was brought there. It was certainly at a cross-point of naval routes. The tendency for comparing it to the other sites on the Armorican continent, as if it were a settlement of 'strangers', would be stretching a point. We have simply there another good example of the 'miracle of conservation'. Mez-Notariou is in a slightly depressed zone with the structures protected by colluvium.

On the mainland, most habitation sites detected up to now (especially those by aerial photography), are towards the top of hills, where soil erosion has been prevailing, so only the deep post-holes or ditches survive. Of course, in the zones where the loessic coat of the northern versant of Brittany was still thick in the Iron Age, not yet eroded away, all traces of settlement sites will have vanished, since quite often several metres of loess have colluviated downslope and gone. We have eloquent information about this erosion with time markers in Bronze Age barrows, and over a century in comparing the present situation and the first detailed geological mapping. Jersey and Guernsey had a nice cover of loess, but with erosion it will have gone down the slopes with so much evidence of the last millenia also.

The 'invasion hypothesis' illness, or its substitutes such as migration or demic diffusion, had not only affected the archaeologists of the British Isles, but also those of the western extremities of mainland Europe. These uttermost ends of the European world being alternatively considered as refuges for residual populations driven back there by the invaders. More romantically, men of letters and poets have imagined peoples such as the 'Celts' riding or driving chariots westward running after the sun and coming against the sea. Of course these Continental populations would have been totally incapable of coping with the ocean. This needs a very long acculturation. The people deserving the name of Armoricae, Amorici or Aremorici must have been for the most of them the descendants of a long inheritance of local populations, possibly and even probably descending from the earliest Mesolithic tribes, with of course continual admission, at least at homoeopathic doses, of their more continental neighbours. This would better explain the several Armorican continuities. Another tendency, favoured by geography, is the crystallization of local small populations in distinctive pagi, a tendency well evident in the XIXth century rural populations - maritime and diverse.

Recent bibliography

P.-R. Giot, J. Briard, L. Pape, *Protohistoire de la Bretagne*. Rennes, Ed. Ouest-France, 1995, 423 p. (revised edition).

About Islands, the collection of the *Bulletin d'information A.M.A.R.A.I. (Association Manche Atlantique pour la Recherche Archéologique dans les Iles)*, Rennes, n° 1, 1988 onwards, one number every year.

Patrimoine archéologique de Bretagne, a series of volumes published from 1989 onwards by the Institut Culturel de Bretagne, Rennes, in co-edition with other societies. For instance: M.-Y. Daire and P.-R. Giot: *1989 Les stèles de l'Age du Fer dans le Léon*, 105 p. (with a text of E. Morel, 1927); J. Y. Robic and others 1992: *L'île d'Ouessant depuis la Préhistoire ... apports de la prospection et de l'archéologie*, 106 p.

Revue archéologique de l'Ouest, Rennes n° 1, 1984 onwards, a volume every year. Also its Supplements such as: *La Bretagne et l'Europe préhistoriques*, n° 2, 1990, 403 p.; *Les Gaulois d'Armorique, la fin de l'Age du Fer en Europe tempérée*, n° 3, 1990, 316 p.; *Paysans et bâtisseurs, l'émergence du Néolithique atlantique et les origines du Mégalithisme*, n° 5, 1992, 262 p.

The *Bulletin de la Société Archéologique du Finistère*, Quimper, every year, is of course the best of the different departmental societies, with good archaeological contributions. More specialized are the *Dossiers du Centre régional d'Archéologie d'Alet*, Saint-Malo, and its supplements, such as: *Un village coriosolite sur l'île des Ebihens (Saint Jacut-de-la-Mer), bilan de trois campagnes de fouilles*, under the direction of L. Langouët, 1989, 173 p.

Among the volumes of the *Travaux du Laboratoire d'Anthropologie*, Université de Rennes I, M.-Y. Daire: *Les céramiques Armoricaines de la fin de l'Age du Fer*, n° 39, 1992 (a doctorate of 1987), 316 p.; D. Marguerie: *Evolution de la végétation sous l'impact humain en Armorique du Néolithique aux périodes historiques*, n° 4, 1992 (a doctorate of 1991), 313 p.; H. Morzadec: *Pétro-Archéologie des céramiques Armoricaines du Néolithique a la fin de l'Age du Fer*, n° 41 (in the press, a doctorate of 1993).

Interim information on the yearly digging seasons of J.-P. Le Bihan at Mez-Notariou on Ouessant can be found in the *Bulletin de la Société Archéologique du Finistére* from 1988 onwards, and in many other publications.

A special item, P.-R. Giot and H. Morzadec: Utilisation préhistorique de la 'metahornblendite' de Pleuven (Finistère): des haches néolithiques à la statu-ette gauloise de Paule Côtes-d'Armor, étude pétroarcheologique, *Comptes-rendus de l'Académie des Sciences*, Paris,t. 315, Série II, pp. 1215-1221, 1992.

Estimation du Volume des Émissions Armoricaines
à partir du trésor de la Marquanderie

BY
KATHERINE GRUEL

Les trésors de monnaies gauloises de Jersey sont apparemment une source inépuisable d'informations pour le protohistorien s'intéressant aux événements de la Guerre des Gaules en Armorique et sur leur conséquence pour l'économie Gallo-Romaine tant en Armorique qu'en Bretagne insulaire. Le trésor de La Marquanderie constitue en particulier une base statistique intéressante pour évaluer le nombre de coins utilisés et estimer le volume des émissions.

J.-B. Colbert de Beaulieu[1] a défini, à partir des trésors de Jersey, une série monétaire, attribuée aux Coriosolites et constituée de sept classes typologiques, pour lesquelles il a proposé une chronologie relative (Fig. 1). L'étude du trésor de Trébry[2], a montré que ces classes s'identifiaient avec des émissions successives. Nous avons eu l'occasion de démontrer que tout portait à penser que les trois dernières classes (classe I, classe III et classe II) correspondaient aux frappes monétaires liées aux événements militaires de 57 et 56 av. J.-C.[3] Si les classes VI, Va, Vb et IV (= groupe 3 de Rybot), au cheval androcéphale bridé au revers, constituent le monnayage Coriosolite, les classes I, III et II seraient beaucoup plus logiquement des émissions de la coalition des cités Armoricaines face à César, que l'atelier monétaire Coriosolite aurait eu la charge de frapper.

Sans reprendre ici toute l'argumentation qui permet d'aboutir à cette conclusion, on rappellera que le trésor de La Marquanderie (Jersey 9) est composé à 99 % de pièces de cette série sur plus de 10,000 monnaies. Ce trésor est considéré comme une part de l'encaisse de l'armée des coalisés Armoricains, battue dans la région d'Avranches par les légions Romaines. Par ailleurs, l'essentiel des monnaies Armoricaines trouvées en Bretagne insulaire appartiennent à cette même série monétaire. Il est donc très possible qu'elles aient servi à payer les mercenaires Bretons appelés à la rescousse par leurs voisins Armoricains[4]. Réunir et entretenir une armée, recruter des mercenaires, tout cela demande de l'argent! Or, une des difficultés rencontrées par les armées Gauloises venait du fait qu'elles combattaient sur leur sol. Cela rendait impossible tout recours au pillage. Les besoins en numéraire devaient donc être importants même si les prélèvements en nature subvenaient à une partie des besoins. Combien les Armoricains ont-ils investi dans la résistance contre Rome? La numismatique permet de chiffrer grossièrement la partie monétaire de la facture de la campagne Armoricaine de 56 av. J.C. Partant de l'étude charactéroscopique des monnaies du trésor de Jersey 9, conservées à la Société Jersiaise, on peut en effet tenter de reconstituer le volume de ces émissions.

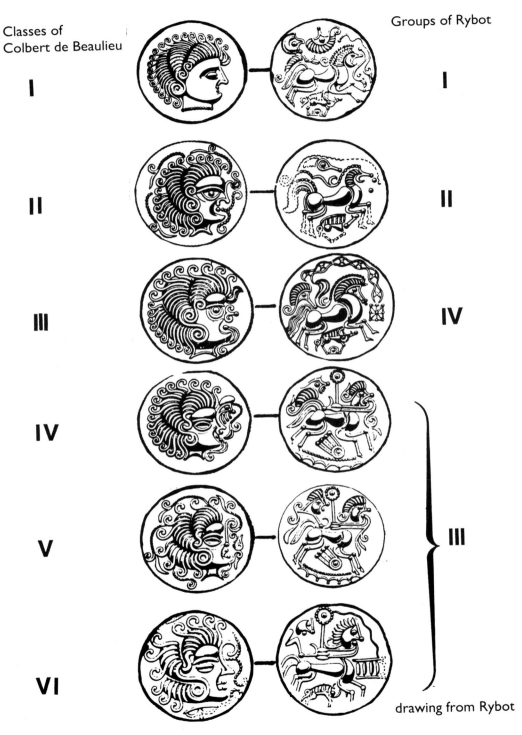

Classes of
Colbert de Beaulieu

Groups of Rybot

drawing from Rybot

Figure. I Classifications of the Coriosolitae Coinage.

Le facies de ce trésor montre de très nombreuses liaisons de coins dans les classes III, I, II, y compris des coins de revers communs à la classe I et III ou à la classe III et II. Ceci permet d'affirmer que la classe III a été frappée entre les classes I et II, que la frappe a été effectuée rapidement, que les pièces ont été peu dispersées avant la thésaurisation. Certains coins de droit sont illustrés par plus de 50 monnaies et, pour la classe II, ce chiffre peut monter jusqu'à 200 pièces par coin.

Les données observées (collection de la Société Jersiaise) sont les suivantes :

Emissions Coriosolites (cheval androcéphale bridé)

Emission	Nbre de Droit	Nbre de Revers	Nbre d'Association	Nbre Monnaies
Classe VI	16	17	21	25
Classe V	91	107	173	285
Classe IV	67	99	232	483

Emissions de la coalition Armoricaine

Emission	Nbre de Droit	Nbre de Revers	Nbre d'Association	Nbre Monnaies
Classe I	66	122	21	1314
Classe III	68	110	99	2053
Classe II	94	non classé	?	4874

En appliquant à ces données les formules mises au point par Carter[5] on obtient une estimation du nombre originel de coins.

Estimation du nombre de coins selon la méthode de Carter avec un écart de confiance de 5% :

Classe	Méthode	Nbre de coins de droits (obverse dies)	Nbre de coins de revers (reverse dies)
VI	Carter	36 +/-9	42 +/-12
V	Carter	113 +/-4	139 +/-6
IV	Carter	70 +/-1	102 +/-2
III	Carter	67 +/-1	100 +/-1
I	Carter	67 +/-1	123 +/-2

Le nombre de coins estimés par cette méthode n'est guère différent des valeurs observées pour les classe III et I. Le nombre de coins estimés pour les revers de la classe III (100) est même inférieur au nombre observé (110) ce qui montre que l'intervalle de confiance retenu est trop faible.

Cependant ces résultats statistiques dans leur imprécision correspondent assez bien à la réalité imaginée par les numismates : en effet, depuis l'étude des coins de droits du trésor de La Marquanderie, aucun nouveau coin des classes I, III et II n'a été identifié. Pourtant, on connaît plus de 30,000 pièces de cette série.

On estime habituellement que le nombre de pièces frappées par coin oscille entre 8,000 et 30,000. Etant donné la dureté des alliages frappées par rapport aux coins de bronze utilisés, nous tablerons sur une production assez basse, disons de 10,000 monnaies par coin de droit. Ceci nous donne les résultats suivants :

Classe VI :	360,000 monnaies
Classe V:	1,130,000 monnaies, à répartir probablement sur 2 émissions, Va et Vb.
Classe IV:	700,000 monnaies
Classe III:	680,000 monnaies
Classe I:	670,000 monnaies

A partir des coins de droits recensés pour la classe II dans le trésor de Jersey 9, on a donc selon ce même calcul simple une émission minimum de 940,000 monnaies, pour 94 coins de droit observés. Ceci donnerait donc un volume minimum d'émissions pour la coalition Armoricaine de 2,290,000 monnaies frappées en 1 ou 2 ans. Par les études de composition effectuées sur cette série monétaire, on peut en fixer l'aloi à cette époque à 1.4 g d'argent par pièce environ . Ceci équivaudrait à une masse minimum d'argent monnayé de 3,206 kg d'argent, pour une campagne de quelques mois.

Les estimations proposées par M. Rousset[6] pour les Classes I et III à partir du trésor de Trébry étaient de 1,900,000 +/- 400,000, soient 1.4 g x 2,000,000= 2,800 kg d'argent . Cette estimation est très proche de celle proposée à partir de Jersey 9. A titre de comparaison, rappelons que, selon Crawford[7], la dépense d'une légion Romaine, en 51 av. J.C., était de 1,500,000 deniers par an. Les deniers Romains ont un aloi de 94% d'argent et pèsent 3.8g. On obtient donc une masse d'argent de 1,500,000 X 3.8g = 5,700 kg d'argent . Cette somme correspond à la somme monnayée nécessaire à l'entretien annuel d'une légion de 5,000 hommes.

Face aux Armoricains coalisés, César envoie trois légions, ce qui doit faire entre 10,000 et 15,000 légionnaires si on tient compte des baisses d'effectifs dues aux décès, aux maladies, ou aux blessures. Il est difficile d'évaluer le nombre de Gaulois rassemblés autour de Viridorix, mais il y a là des contingents des Unelli, des Coriosolites, des Lexovii et des Aulerques Eburovices (César, 3, XI, 4). Si nous reprenons les chiffres demandés pour l'armée envoyée au secours Vercingétorix, quâtre ans plus tard, les cités Armoricaines étaient sensées pouvoir encore mobiliser 26,000 hommes (César, 7, LXXV). Il n'est donc pas irrationnel d'estimer l'armée terrestre Armoricaine de 56 av. J.-C. à plusieurs dizaines de milliers d'hommes d'autant plus que César en souligne le grand nombre (César, 3, XVII, 2). De plus, il semble que l'armée de Viridorix comptaient en plus non seulement des mercenaires Bretons mais aussi des "guerriers de fortune" venus de toute la Gaule (César, 3, XVII, 4). La bataille tourna court en faveur des Romains, avant la distribution de la solde comme en témoignent les nombreux trésors Coriosolites qui tracent les lignes de fuite des Gaulois à partir de la région d'Avranches, d'une part par mer vers Jersey, d'autre part par terre, vers l'Ouest[8].

    A qui était destiné cet argent monnayé par les Coriosolites pour l'armée Armoricaine. La comparaison avec les comptes des légions Romaines tendrait à prouver que cette somme n'est pas suffisante pour rémunérer la totalité de l'armée de Viridorix. On peut par ailleurs admettre que les contingents "réguliers" des cités Gauloises engagées dans la révolte n'étaient pas payés puisqu'ils défendaient leur territoire. En revanche, les mercenaires et "les guerriers de fortune" dont parle César l'étaient sûrement. Ces émissions particulièrement abondantes de la coalition Armoricaine ont servi à les rétribuer, partie avant la bataille comme le veut l'usage, partie après. Cette seconde partie ne put être distribuée pour cause de défaite et correspondrait aux trésors Coriosolites, en particulier à ceux de Jersey. Une des traces de la première partie serait les découvertes de monnaies Armoricaines quasi exclusivement de ce type en Bretagne insulaire, témoignage du retour des mercenaires Bretons engagés en 56 av.J.-C.

    Il est difficile de faire parler davantage ces chiffres déjà approximatifs: A combien revenait l'embauche de chaque mercenaire? 1 kg d'argent comme un légionnaire Romaine? Plus? Moins? Difficile à dire. Tout l'argent monnayé à cet effet a-t-il été engagé dès le départ ? Probablement. Tout cet argent a-t-il été versé? Assurément non. On peut d'ailleurs probablement voir dans l'existence de cette masse monétaire existante, une des raisons de la prospérité de la cité Coriosolite d'Alet après la conquête Romaine et un des facteurs du développement du commerce trans-Manche entre Alet et Hengisbury Head, ce monnayage ayant alors cours des deux côtés de la Manche.

1.   J.-B. Colbert de Beaulieu, 1973, *Traité de Numismatique Celtique*, Paris

2.   K. Gruel, 1981, *Le trésor de Trébry*, Paris

3.   César, *De Bello Gallico*, livre 3, année 56 av. J.C.

4.   K. Gruel, 1989, *La monnaie chez les Gaulois*, Paris

5.   G. F. Carter, 1980, *A graphical method for calculating the approximate total number of dies from die-link statistic of Ancient Coins*, in W. A. Oddy (ed), Studies in Numismatics, pp 17-29

6.   M. Rousset, 1987, *Possibilités de l'étude des liaisons de coins, Mélanges Colbert de Beaulieu,* Paris 7 pp 733-742

7.   M. H. Crawford, 1974, *Roman Republic Coinage*, Cambridge, p 633 et ss.

8.   K. Gruel, M. Barral, M. Veillon, Aleas de la frappe monétaire `a l'époque gauloises in *Rythmes de la production monétaire de l'Antiquité à nos jours*, G. Depeyrot, G. Mowcharte, T. Hackens (ed) Louvain-La -Neuve, 1987 pp 174-186

An estimate of the volume of some Armorican Coin Issues

on the basis of the La Marquanderie hoard

BY

KATHERINE GRUEL

English summary

The hoards of Gaulish coins found in Jersey provide a valuable source of information concerning the Roman conquest of Armorica and its economic and social consequences. The La Marquanderie hoard, containing more than 10,000 coins almost solely of the Coriosolitae, provides a particularly useful basis from which to calculate the number of dies and estimate the volume of the issue.

The Coriosolite series is divided into seven typological classes, of which the three latest types (class I, III and II) seem to relate to the military events of 57 and 56 BC, and specifically to the production by the Coriosolitae of a coinage on behalf of the Armorican coalition. The La Marquanderie hoard can be considered as part of the reserves of this coalition, defeated in the Avranches region by the Roman army.

The study of the La Marquanderie hoard shows numerous die-links between classes III, I and II, consisting of reverse dies linking classes I and III or classes III and II. This indicates that class III was struck between classes I and II, that the coinage was struck quickly, and that there was little time for it to be dispersed. Some obverse dies are represented by more than 50 coins, and for class II the figure can reach 200 coins per die.

The estimates of the original number of dies in use which can be calculated from these figures correspond fairly well to the totals expected by numismatists, for example an estimate of 100 reverse dies for class III, in comparison with an observed figure of 110. No new dies have been identified since the study of the La Marquanderie hoard.

Estimates of the numbers of coins struck per die vary considerably. On the basis of a figure of 10,000 coins per obverse die, this suggests a minimum number of 2,290,000 coins struck in the space of one or two years for the Armorican coalition, using more than 3,200 kg. of silver. However in comparison with the silver necessary to pay a Roman legion this seems an inadequate amount to support the Armorican forces commanded by Viridorix against the Roman army. It is possible that the issues for the Armorican coalition were intended specifically for mercenaries (including Britons) rather than for native Armoricans, although it is impossible to say how much each mercenary received.

The Coriosolite hoards, particularly on Jersey, represent that part of the coinage which could not be distributed following the defeat of the Armorican forces. It is possible that the existence of this mass of coinage was one of the factors behind the prosperity of the Coriosolite port of Alet after the conquest, and the development of cross-Channel trade between Alet and Hengistbury Head, the coinage being recognised and accepted on both sides of the Channel.

Roman Pottery from the Bonded Store, St. Peter Port
A Preliminary View

BY

JASON MONAGHAN

Excavations at the Bonded Store, St Peter Port, were in progress as this brief report was written. Four trenches were initially opened, two in Area 'A', the lower part of the store and two in Area 'B' below the market halls. Only pottery from Area A will be considered. Here, after removal of the chalk floor of the Victorian building, excavations immediately revealed deposits which contained primarily Roman material. All layers contained small quantities of 19th century pottery, glass and bricks dating to the time of the construction of the store. This construction seems to have truncated any deposits which date between the 4th and 19th centuries, as there was precious little medieval pottery found.

This report is a short summary of the Roman material found in January and February 1996 from contexts which were probably re-deposited. It therefore includes no illustration or references and only partial quantification. The pottery is indicative of what has been previously found in Guernsey, mainly being of Gallic origin with additional sources in southern England and amphoras from as far away as Spain.

No pottery was found which had dates confined to the first century AD, although the date span of some vessels begins this early. Significantly there was none of the common Flavian fine wares such as Lyons ware and no South Gaulish Samian, which would be expected if there was occupation prior to AD 110.

Samian

This was a mixture of Central and East Gaulish fabrics, dating from c.AD 120 through to the middle of the third century. Forms included Curle 23, Ludowici Tg, Dragendorff 31R, 33, 37, 43 and 45. One stamp was sent for examination by Brenda Dickinson of Leeds University and shown to be of Cobnertianus.

Oxidised wares

These included a 'legionary' style carinated bowl with reeded rim, dated from the Augustan period on the Continent and thought obsolete by c.AD 120 in Britain. This is usually but not exclusively found on military sites. A hemispherical bowl imitating Samian form Drag. 37 and the neck of a 'pulley wheel' flagon were also found; these are usually mid-late second century.

Gallo-Roman Grey wares

The principal grey ware had a soft, sandy fabric and dark grey-black coloration, typical of the Gallo-Roman tradition of the region. A grey foot may have been from a tripod bowl of Gallic origin dating to the second or third century. Fine grey sherds with roulette decoration would be from beakers, again probably Gallic. Two sherds were of North Gaulish Grey ware, one being of a second century 'vase tronconique ' and the other a rim either from a similar vessel or from a third century pentice-moulded beaker. The base of what was probably another pentice-moulded beaker was also found in cream-grey fabric.

Romano-British coarsewares

Several sherds of Dorset BB1 were noted, including the rim of a third-century cooking pot and part of a decorated dish base. Some light-cored sherds may be of Alice Holt origin.

Traded Fine wares

One sherd of Cologne colour-coated ware was from a 'bag beaker' with part of the decoration suggestive of a mid-2nd century 'hunt cup'. Two sherds were of Trier 'Moselkeramik'; one a globular beaker, one a folded beaker, dating from c. AD 190 through to c.AD 250.

Amphorae

Few amphora sherds were discovered. One body sherd would have been from a Dressel 20 Spanish olive-oil amphora. One flat base was found of 'Gauloise' type, plus a reeded rim from a further, second-century, example. The remaining sherds were also of Gallic origin.

Mortaria

Apart from two sherds of Samian forms 43 and 45, the only mortarium was of parchment ware, possibly of the New Forest industries, with the remains of red decoration above its flange, which was broken off. This is the latest piece immediately identifiable and would date to the late third or fourth centuries.

Sherd count Area A.

	Area 1	Area 2	Area 2 (%)
Coarse Oxidised wares	8	82	27%
Coarse Grey wares	15	57	19%
Local gallo-Roman	6	54	18%
Fine grey wares	3	48	16%
Samian	8	33	11%
'white' flagons	1	16	5%
Black burnished BB1	3	5	2%
Colour coated ware	0	5	2%
Amphorae	3	2	< 1%
Mortaria	0	1	< 1%
	47	303	100%

Area B contained an additional 140 small scraps of coarseware of c. less than 1g weight, whilst Area A contained 12.

Roman Tile	Area B only
Tegula sherds	42
Imbrex sherds	14
Tile scraps	43

Conclusions

It is clear that the excavation is in the near vicinity of a Roman building; this either lay below the Bonded Store/markets or was a short distance away, possibly closer to the Church. Roman material is fairly homogeneous, with a number of match-breaks and is not mixed with medieval pottery. This suggests that re-deposition of the material followed quickly on disturbance. The tile likewise is in large pieces. Roman occupation in the area seems to have begun in the early second century and continued perhaps to the fourth. At 11%, the quantity of Samian is perhaps at the level one would expect from an urban domestic site. The majority of vessels are coarseware jars, with a typical kitchen suite of lids, beakers, bowls and flagons. The shortage of amphorae argues against the building being a warehouse: it was not the Roman equivalent of the Bonded Store!

German Salt-glazed Stoneware bottle with face mask. From the late 16th Century Shipwreck off Alderney
Photograph Michael Bowyer.

Excavations at Kings Road, St. Peter Port, Guernsey in 1983

Excavations at Lihou Priory Guernsey in 1990.
Directed by Bob Burns

Frederick Corbin Lukis
1788 - 1871

Members of La Société Guernesiaise visiting the site
of L'Islet Cist - In- Circles in 1912

Excavations on Les Fouaillages, Guernsey 1981

A group of unstratified Clay Pipes and Bowls

from the seabed off St Peter Port, Guernsey

BY

NICKY A DAVID

This article is dedicated to Bob Burns, without whose help and encouragement I would never have started or persevered with the study of clay pipes.

As well as diving to specific wrecks and underwater archaeological sites, members of the Guernsey Nautical Archaeological Team (GNAT) sometimes retrieve loose unstratified material from the sea bed. The following is a record of two groups of clay tobacco pipes collected by the team, the first, Group A, from a gully in the rocks on the North-East side of Castle Cornet in December 1987, and the second, Group B. from the bed of St Peter Port Harbour mouth in the spring of 1994. (Fig 1)

St. Peter Port
showing the sites
of clay pipe deposits

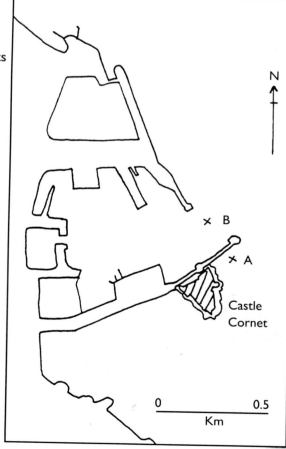

Figure 1

Key
A.   Gully in rocks on
N E side of
Castle Cornet
B.   New Harbour
Mouth

Although normally unstratified, clay pipes from underwater sites have an important place in archaeological research. (Higgins, D A, 1995). They provide evidence, or support of documentary evidence, of trade in clay pipes and other commodities, and can provide accurate dating information particularly when found in association with identifiable wrecks.

Group A consists of 10 unused bowls and bowl fragments together with a number of unmarked stem fragments all of the same form and probably from the same mould. It is therefore likely that they were from a cargo deposit rather than sporadic deposits from different provenances. The pipes have a bowl type with a dating of 1700-1720 and a style produced in the Southampton, Portsmouth, and Salisbury regions. Similar pipes were found during excavations at Castle Cornet, (David, N A, forthcoming), and these could well have been part of a cargo of supplies to the Castle or to the Town of St Peter Port.

Group B consists of 21 complete or nearly complete bowls representing 20 different pipes with a date range of 1670-1880. They include decorated pipes and several with identifiable makers' marks, representing trade from English south coast ports, and the Netherlands. As there are only two identical pipes in this group, it seems that these finds are likely to be sporadic deposits, either thrown overboard from ships or with the town's rubbish. Some show evidence of having been smoked and are more likely to be discarded used products than lost cargo. The pipes in both groups are very water-worn with many of the decorative features only partly identifiable. Nevertheless, they provide important evidence of the known trading routes to Guernsey, and a record of the destination of some clay pipe products.

What at first sight appears to be an insignificant group of unstratified archaeological finds, does in fact enhance existing knowledge by providing increased information about imported products and their provenance. As further pipe groups are excavated, studied, and documented, from both land and nautical sites, this knowledge will hopefully be increased further.

Catalogue

Group A. Pipe material from Gully, NE side of Castle Cornet. (Fig 2.)

It comprised
1 Complete bowl
6 Incomplete bowls Date range 1700-1720
3 Bowl fragments
18 Unmarked stem fragments (including several long lengths up to 12.5cm)
Brittle spurred bowls, plain rims parallel to stem.

Type produced by many 18th century makers in Southern England including the Sayer and Potell families of Fareham (Fox, R T and Hall, R B 1979), William Ally, Isle of Wight (Fox, R and Barton, K J 1986) and Sidney family, Southampton (Vincent, J 1993). Pipes of these makers have been found at Castle Cornet (David, N A, forthcoming).

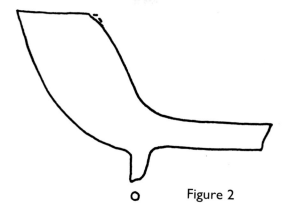

Figure 2

Group B. Scattered pipe material from the mouth of St Peter Port Harbour. (Figs. 3-6)

It comprised
21 Complete or near-complete bowls
1 Bowl/stem fragment
5 Unmarked stem fragments, up to 17.5cm in length

Date range 1670-1880, all water-worn, obliterating mouldings and relief markings.

1   1670-1700   Southern/SW style. White fabric, rim rouletted.

2   1680-1720   London/Southern style. Rim partly rouletted.

3   1690- 1710   London/SE style. Thick-walled bowl, plain rim.

4   1690- 1710   London/Southern style with spur and rouletted rim.

5-6   1720-1760   Southern/SW styles. Spurred type with plain rim.

7   1750-1770   Dutch pipe. Burnished bowl with rouletting around rim. Spur partly missing. Small circular relief mark on right side of spur -? a mould mark (See Duco, D 1987)

8   1760-1780   Dutch pipe. Large burnished bowl with rouletted rim. Product of Gouda. Shield mark of Gouda pipemaker on sides of spur. Relief letter S above the shield denotes an ordinary quality pipe. (Duco, D 1987) Base has an unidentified crowned relief mark

9   1775-1810   Ribbed bowl with initials AC in relief on sides of spur. Product of Arthur Coster of Fareham. Parallels at Portsmouth (Fox, R and Barton, K J 1986) and Castle Cornet.

10   1780-1810   Armorial bowl bearing Prince of Wales feathers in relief on the left side of the bowl and the royal arms of Hanover on the right. 'Arrow' leaf pattern along front mould line. The Unicorn is a common design of this period.

11   1790-1820 Badly worn example of brittle spurred bowl bearing ? the Royal Arms with rampant supporters in relief on the back of the bowl, leaf pattern along front mould line.

12   1750-1800 Brittle ribbed bowl. Initials II in relief on side of square spur. Possible maker John Jones of Carisbrooke, Isle of Wight, listed as aged 80 in 1841 census. (Oswald, A, 1975).

13- 15 Products of Thomas Frost of Southampton who produced pipes from 1803-39. Relief initials TF on sides of spur.

13   'Trafalgar' pipe depicting Nelson and Britannia in relief moulding on the sides of the bowl. Commemorating the Battle of Trafalgar 1805.

14   Ribbed pattern.

15   Bearing arms of Southampton and a detailed stalk and leaf pattern along the front mould line

16   1800-40 Ribbed and swag pattern. Relief spur initials T ? ? Thomas Frost cf 13- 15 above.

17   1840-70 Ribbed style. Relief initials GH on side of spur. Probably the product of George Harding who is listed as a pipemaker in the Southampton directories 1843-67 (Oswald, A, 1975).

18-19   1850-80 Small spurred pipes with relief decorations. No makers' marks. 18 has ribbed and swag pattern. 19 has leaf pattern along mould lines.

20   Extremely eroded specimen with spur missing. Evidence of relief decoration of a ship's anchor on both sides of bowl, a popular design of c 1850.

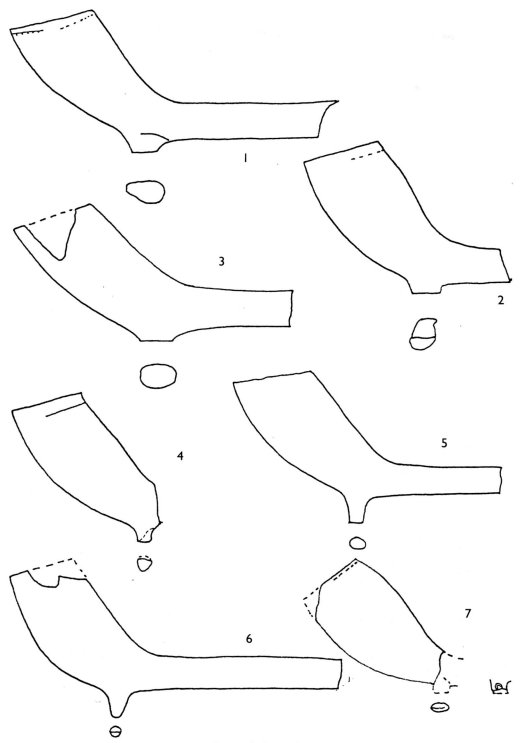

Figure 3. Scale 1:1

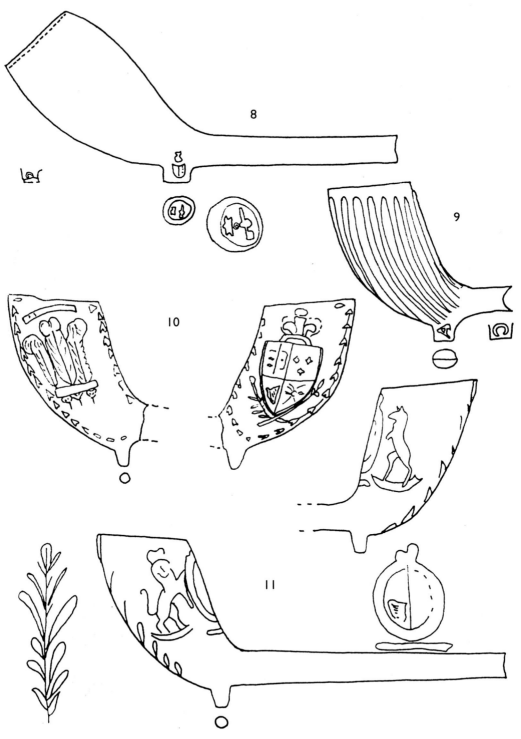

Figure 4. Scale 1:1

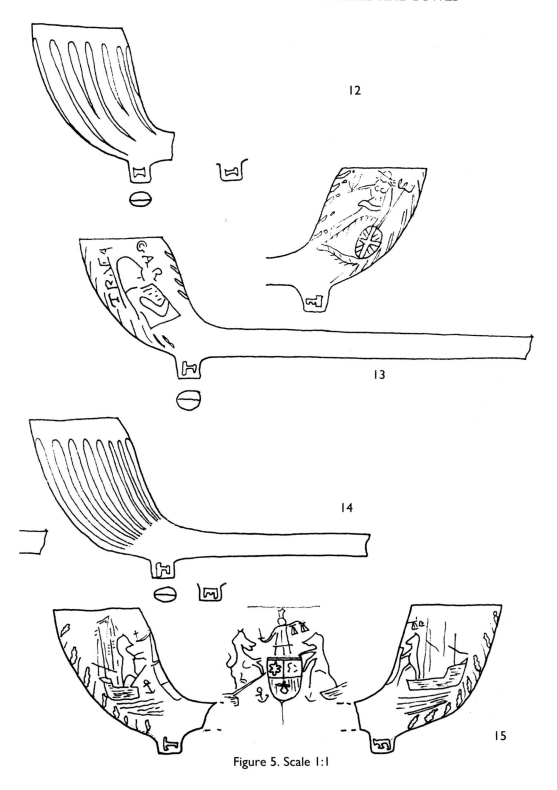

Figure 5. Scale 1:1

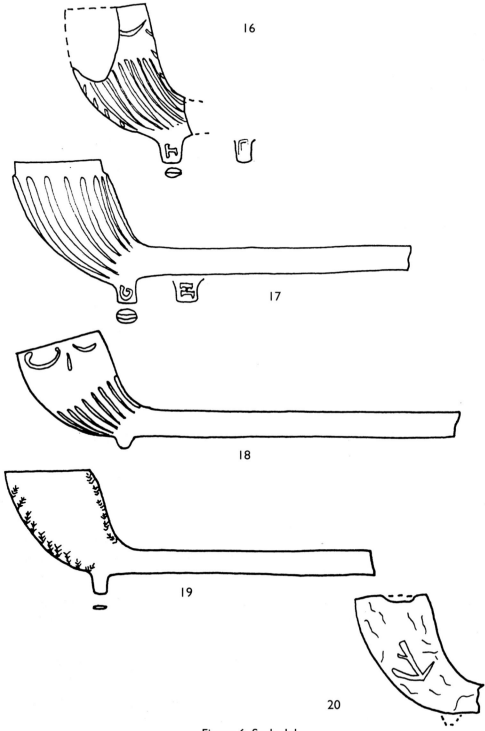

Figure 6. Scale 1:1

Acknowledgement

My thanks to the Guernsey Nautical Archaeological team for allowing me to study these pipes and publish my findings.

References

David, N A, (forthcoming) 'The clay tobacco pipes' in *Excavations at Castle Cornet, Barton, K J, (forthcoming)*

Duco, D, 1987, *De Nederlandse Kleipijp*, pub Pijpenkabinet, Leiden, Netherlands.

Fox, R T and Hall, R B, 1979, *The Clay Tobacco Pipes of the Portsmouth Harbour Region 1680- 1932*. Portsmouth City Museums

Fox, R and Barton, K J, 1986, 'Excavations at Oyster Street, Portsmouth, Hants, 1968-71' In *Post Mediaeval Archaeology*, Vol 20, pp 31 -255.

Higgins, D A., 1995, 'Clay Tobacco Pipes: a valuable commodity.' *International Journal of Nautical Archaeology*, Vol 24.1 pp 47-52.

Oswald, A., 1975, 'Clay Pipes for the Archaeologist.' *British Archaeological Reports* 14.

Vincent, J, 1993, Southampton City Museum service, Pers. Comm.

Additional Bibliography

Atkinson, D ., 1970, 'Clay Tobacco Pipes and Pipemakers of Salisbury, Wilts'. *Wiltshire Archaeological and Natural History Magazine*, No 65, pp 177- 189 .

Atkinson, D R, and Oswald, A, 1972, 'A Brief Guide to the Identification of Dutch Clay Tobacco Pipes found in England.' *Post- Mediaeval Archaeology*, Vol 6 pp l75-182.

Atkinson, D ., 1975, *The Clay Tobacco Pipes in Excavations in Mediaeval Southampton 1953-69*, Vol 2, by C Platt and R Coleman-Smith. Leicester University Press.

Atkinson, D R, and Oswald, A, 'The Dating and Typology of clay pipes bearing the Royal Arms.' *Archaeology of the Clay Pipe III*. British Archaeological Reports 78.

Duco, D H, 1982, *Merken van Goudse Pijpen makers 1660-1940*. Pijpenkabinet, Netherlands.

Le Cheminant, R, 1981, 'Clay Pipes bearing the Prince of Wales' Feathers.' *Archaeology of the Clay Tobacco Pipe VI*. British Archaeological Reports 97.

Medieval Peasant Buildings In Brittany:
oval and rectangular, plans and uses.

BY

MICHAEL BATT

In Brittany from the Neolithic to the end of the Iron Age there is a paucity of information in the archaeological record concerning house types. For the shorter medieval period however, peasant buildings are relatively well known. Grouped either in small nucleated settlements or sometimes isolated in the landscape, the surviving sites are mostly situated on what is today (and almost certainly was in the Middle Ages) marginal land of the interior uplands or on the coast. The number of sites which have been located and excavated in recent years tends to obscure the fact that, before 1969, the little medieval archaeology that existed was mostly carried out by art historians. It was almost entirely concerned with the study of standing buildings erected by the wealthier members of the population: principally ecclesiastical buildings, castles and manor houses. Apart from work carried out on Ile Guennoc during the 1950s (Giot, 1982), there is little record of any scientific excavation having been carried out in Brittany on medieval peasant buildings. Not that such sites had escaped the notice of 19th century antiquarians; explorations during the 1890s in the Monts d'Arrée, Finistère (du Chatellier, 1907, pp 235-237) revealed the existence of one settlement (Karhaes Vihan, Brennillis) situated in close proximity to a group of Bronze Age barrows and considered at that time to be contemporary in date with them. More recently excavations on the site between 1978 and 1985 have confirmed that this settlement is medieval. At the beginning of the 20th century the publication of a study of pre-Roman settlements in the Morbihan notes in particular one deserted settlement (Lann Gouh, Melrand) as being *'une cité armoricaine au temps des celtes'* (Granciere, 1902). Excavations carried out on this site since 1977 have also confirmed this settlement to be of the medieval period.

In 1969, on the Atlantic coast some 250 metres from the sea, at Guidel near Lorient, Morbihan, sand extraction from coastal dunes uncovered the remains of a medieval settlement comprising at least seven buildings, known as Pen- er- Malo. Only three buildings were examined archaeologically. All were oval in plan, the gable end walls being apsidal, and one building being dated by coin evidence to the 12th century (Bertrand and Lucas, 1975). This discovery was followed by others, this time in the interior uplands of the Morbihan at Kérlano, Plumelec and at Lesturgant, Malguenac (Andre, 1976) where oval plan buildings were also identified. It was between 1969 and 1972 that the study of peasant buildings started to receive the necessary attention from Breton archaeologists, with work on deserted medieval settlements reaching its peak in the region between 1972 and 1985.

These early discoveries in the Morbihan of medieval buildings, oval in plan with apsidal gables, received swift attention from Breton and non-Breton archaeologists. For some time it was thought that they represented the house type of medieval rural Brittany, a model persisting from that period until the first quarter of the 20th century (Chapelot and Fossier, 1980, pp 234-5). Subsequent excavation soon indicated that the picture was not so simple. Buildings, oval and rectangular in plan were found coexisting not only in the same region but also on the same site, some buildings even bearing both oval and rectangular characteristics.

Nine medieval settlements of the earlier and later medieval periods have been excavated in Brittany since 1969 thus giving sufficient information to enable some general conclusions to be drawn on Breton medieval peasant house types and comparisons to be made with similar structures outside the region.

Breton medieval settlements can be divided both chronologically and geographically into two distinct zones: Upper Brittany, to the east, where settlements and buildings were realised in perishable materials and are largely earlier than 1,000 AD; Lower Brittany, to the west, where settlements and buildings were in stone and mostly later than 1,000 AD.

The earliest excavations were carried out in Lower Brittany on the post AD 1,000 sites, which were studied either by simple trenching or by more consequential programmed research excavations. By 1980 a series of well structured deserted settlements had been examined, the ruined walls being easily identifiable before excavation as low banks and hollows on uncultivated heathland. The most important result of these excavations has been to demonstrate that the simple longhouse, which is widely known in the existing vernacular architecture tradition (Meirion-Jones, 1973), was common, and was to be found in Brittany during the medieval period at least as early as the 12th century. In all excavated buildings the walls were constructed using the dry-stone technique with locally quarried or surface collected stone, mainly granite, clay and/or earth bonding being wide-spread. It is reasonable to assume that the roofs of buildings were covered with some form of organic material such as broom, a cheap material used until recently on primitive rural architecture.

More recently the results of rescue excavations, mostly undertaken in Upper Brittany, are now starting to fill in gaps in our knowledge concerning the period earlier than AD 1,000. By contrast with the post-AD 1,000 period, we are dealing here with buildings constructed entirely from perishable materials, so evidence is based on the traces left by timber uprights placed in separate postholes or continuous foundation trenches.

For this earlier period, the partial plan of an aisled structure based on posthole alignments was revealed by excavation in 1986 at Crec'h Gwen, Quimper, Finistere (Menez and Batt, 1987), and in 1989 at Le Cocherais, Tinteniac, Ille-et-Vilaine, where no building plans were identified, but hearths, ovens, storage pits and property boundaries indicate the existence of a very important early medieval settlement (Le Boulanger, Provost and Leroux 1992). Amongst more recent discoveries in Ille-et-Vilaine, not yet fully published, is a multi-period site excavated in 1993 only some two kilometres from the centre of Rennes on the site of a new sewage treatment plant at Beaurade. Here tantalising evidence of early medieval occupation was found, again hearths, pits and post-holes indicating the presence of a small riverside settlement. At Janzé, Ille-et-Vilaine much clearer evidence has been forthcoming: complete plans of post built structures were brought to light during recent excavations in 1994. All three sites excavated in Ille-et-Vilaine have their beginnings before AD 1,000. None of these were known before excavation, their discovery being due entirely to careful and intensive assessment work carried out before major road building or construction projects. Local geological conditions mean that none were discovered by aerial photography, and intensive agriculture over the last 1,000 years has no doubt eliminated any standing earthworks. This explains why so few of these sites are known and why they are so hard to find. In the future, rescue archaeology will no doubt be an important source of information, not only for archaeology and the study of building evolution in general, and it will almost certainly change our vision of the history of medieval landscape usage. It is not possible to say more about these sites at present, and we must now wait for their definitive publication.

It is now clear after more than twenty-five years research that these early excavations indicate the coexistence of two house types during the medieval period in Brittany; both oval and rectangular, both corresponding to types defined by British archaeologists during the last twenty - five years (Beresford and Hurst, 1971,pp 104 ff and fig 17; Austin 1985).

The existence of oval buildings in Brittany has for long been considered as a purely regional phenomenon. Why did they emerge here ? Many cohabit with rectangular structures on the same settlement. Without any doubt these structures can be classed as elementary longhouses (Meirion-Jones, 1973). They bear some or all of the internal characteristics necessary; a living area heated by a central hearth, a byre or stable, opposed doors, cooking pits and annexe rooms. The existence of longhouses, both oval and rectangular, tends to imply an all year round occupation; the walls being of stone, only the roof would need a permanent supervision of the fabric. We may assume therefore that the average life-span of these buildings was expected to be long: perhaps two or three generations at least.

At this stage it would be useful to pose the following questions: do oval buildings present any architectural advantages over rectangular structures? Does the oval plan reply to any particular architectural problem? Are they a response to some particular lack in building materials such as wood for roof carpentry? Are they more wind resistant? No antecedents are known in Brittany before or during Roman period, the architecture of the latter period falling into the rigid mould imposed on Gaul.

The most well known and published example of an oval building is building A at Pen-er-Malo, Guidel, Morbihan. It is a good example of a simple longhouse comprising a central hearth, opposing doors (one blocked during a later phase) and a low internal wall separating the (?) byre from the living area (fig 1). Other published oval structures are similar in plan and construction techniques do not differ greatly. Examples are numerous in the Morbihan as at Lesturgant, Malguénac (fig 2,1) and Kerlano, Plumelec (fig 2,2) (Andre, Bertrand and Clement 1976). New sites coming to light in other departments as in Finistère at Ergue-Gaberic (fig 3,1) (Tinevez and Pennec, 1985) and more recently in the Côtes d'Armor at Coz Yaudet, Ploul'ech (Galliou and Cunliffe, 1995). Outside Brittany, oval buildings are rare but not unknown. At Bretteville-sur-Laize, Calvados, during the excavation of a small ringwork a small oval building was uncovered (fig 3,2). While no central hearth was observed it is similar in plan to the oval buildings of the Morbihan (Decaens, 1968). It is at present the only example known in lower Normandy. Outside continental France, two complete and one practically destroyed oval buildings (fig 3,3) were excavated on the west coast of Guernsey in 1986 at Le Port aux Malades (Burns and Batt, 1990). They are small simple oval longhouses, comparable to those of Pen-er-Malo, building 1 having a central hearth, and building 2 an internal dividing wall separating the living area from the possible byre end. As at Pen-er-Malo the site is situated a short distance from the sea, suggesting perhaps a mixed economy based on the exploitation of the sea and land. However, apart from these architectural similarities no other comparisons are possible. Not surprisingly the ceramic evidence places this Channel Island site culturally in Normandy and not in Brittany. Many are those who would have liked to have seen this site as a Breton colony!

But are these oval buildings purely medieval and represented only in north western France? No thorough bibliographical research has yet been undertaken but one can already pin-point a certain number of examples which are pre-Roman or post-medieval in date and situated outside the area which concerns us here. An oval building was excavated in 1988 at the Oppidum of Gailhan in the Var, situated some 30 kilometres north east of Montpellier in southern France (fig 3,4) (Dedet, 1990). Measuring internally some 8.20 metres by 3.70 to 3.80 metres, this building has been dated by artefacts to the mid fifth century BC and presents many elements found in medieval Breton oval buildings: hearths, dividing walls etc... Other buildings of this type dated also to the 6th and 5th centuries BC are known elsewhere in southern France mainly along the Languedoc coast. For the moment it would be unwise to try to make any comparison with any of the medieval Breton examples discussed above for one is walking here on dangerous ground. Medieval and post-medieval oval buildings are surprisingly even more difficult to locate in the literature. In this region of the Languedoc, Roussillon a medieval building with one apsidal gable was excavated on the commune of Saint Martin de Londres, Herault, and dated by ceramic evidence not later than the 12th century (Gasco1983). Until recently no excavated examples of oval or apsidal gable buildings were known on the upland areas of the Limousin. However, recent field work has now brought to light about two dozen deserted settlements in the Montagne Limousine, Corrèze, of which three have been studied archaeologically. Oval buildings are now known at, la Grange de Cournille, Saint Cernin de Larche (Conte, 1988), at the Bois des Brigands, Valièrgues (Conte, 1993) and at the Cousage, Chasteaux (Gady, 1993). All these structures are medieval, dated by ceramic evidence to the 13th-15th centuries. Surveys of vernacular architecture have revealed at the same time that a certain number of post medieval buildings, mostly barns, with apsidal gabled walls, exist and are not rare. (Bans and Bans 1979).

While no excavated examples are known for the medieval period in the region of Limoges, surveys of vernacular architecture have revealed that a certain number of post medieval buildings, mostly barns, with apsidal gabled walls, exist and are not rare (Bans and Bans 1979).

This brief look at the problem of oval buildings brings to light the necessity of serious bibliographical work on such structures. How common are they? What is our knowledge of such structures during the prehistoric and pre-Roman and medieval periods? How widespread are these structures throughout France and Europe?

The cohabitation of oval structures with the more traditional rectangular buildings is well illustrated on Breton sites especially in the Morbihan, particularly on the sites of Lann-Goh, Melrand (fig 4) and the Forest of Pont Calleck, Berné (fig 5). Excavated examples of rectangular buildings are numerous in both the Morbihan and Finistère. Enough examples have now been excavated for us to speak of an evolution from the simple longhouse with central hearth, opposing doors and light divisions between the living and the byre areas, such as at Lann-Goh, Melrand, and to compare them with those in Finistère on such sites as Karhaes Vihan, Brennilis (fig 6) (Batt, 1990, pp 19-20) and Le Goënidou, Berrien (figs 7 and 8) (Barrere and Batt 1990, pp 19). On both these sites more evolved structures have now been excavated. The preliminary field survey in 1984 at Le Goënidou permitted the identification of at least three groups or units of buildings each comprising four constructions. The disposition of the buildings in each group or unit is identical, suggesting a deliberate laying out of this settlement to a preconceived plan: three buildings grouped around a courtyard, a fourth being situated a short distance away. Excavation has confirmed this and indicates that no major reorganisation of the site has occurred since it was originally laid out. Such a regular organisation would suggest that this settlement was a deliberate implantation, probably at the initiative of a powerful local land owner. In this particular case the Cistercians of the nearby Abbey of Le Relecq would seem to be the most likely candidates. They had their own particular form of land tenure known as the quévaise, its purpose being to attract settlers to recently colonised land. Sufficient evidence is now available as a result of excavation on this site to allow us to interpret these buildings. Buildings 1 and 2 (fig 6) are longhouses, presenting not only the traditional central hearth but also shelves and cupboards constructed in the stone walls and clear separations between the living area and the byre, the latter having a separate doorway for animals. The internal separation still has no structural function apart from it being a support for a light division probably in wattle and daub. An annexe room, another innovation, is accessible only from the living area. While necessity continued to compel man to live under the same roof as his livestock there are now clear signs indicating a wish to live separately from his beasts. This desire to live separately from the livestock is further confirmed by the existence of building 2(fig 7) and a similar building (not illustrated). Despite their similarity in size and construction, the excavation results indicate non-domestic functions (absence of central hearths) such as byres or barns. The presence of outhouses and important non-domestic buildings at Karhaes Vihan and at Le Goënidou are perhaps signs of an increase in livestock numbers. These additions are probably a result of an increase in the general prosperity of these settlements due to improved farming techniques being imposed by the land-owners: in the case of Le Goenidou (if our assumptions are correct) the monks of Le Relecq. The area occupied by the living area does not however increase in general so dramatically if we compare that of house A at Pen-er-Malo and that of buildings 1 and 3 (fig 7) at Le Goenidou. The more evolved architecture of the site of Le Goënidou has much in common with that present on the upland sites of south west England such as Houndtor and Hutholes (Beresford 1979) or the upland steading at Beere, North Tawton (Jope and Threlfall, 1958) where an economy based on pastoralism is well attested.

The excavation of what now amounts to half a dozen medieval deserted settlements has revealed a series of peasant buildings, oval and rectangular in plan, dated broadly on the present evidence to the period between the 12th and 14th centuries. It is generally felt that the vast majority of the excavated stone structures of the region are roughly contemporary, an assumption which is for the moment difficult to accept or refute considering the absence of solid dating evidence. Numismatic evidence is absent on all sites apart from Pen-er-Malo where four coins were discovered during excavation, three of which were of Conan III (1112-1148) while the fourth was illegible. There is little stratigraphy on these sites and it would appear for the moment that pottery types change little over several hundred years in the peasant settlements of Brittany. Our main problem is the imprecision of the chronology of these sites and their buildings. This problem is also heightened by an absence of detailed archive work on each individual site which would enable us to understand the reasons behind the creation and eventual desertion of such settlements in the landscape of medi-eval Brittany. The communities that lived, worked and died in these settlements scratched an existence out of the surrounding land, their economy based on mixed agriculture. We have little or no evidence that would give us reliable answers on population numbers, but we can perhaps assume that each longhouse represented at least one family unit. These communities were not isolated from the outside world; while there is a marked absence of coins, the presence of ceramic, albeit of low quality, confirms the existence of contacts with local markets.

Therefore, despite a large amount of excavation undertaken on medieval deserted settlements several questions remain. What were the factors behind the creation of these settlements and their buildings? Why did an oval architecture emerge? Perhaps a new series of programmed excavations related to fieldwork associated with detailed documentary and environmental studies should be considered.

Many thanks are due to Deidre McKeown who read and corrected this text and to Jean-Pierre Bardel who provided access to unpublished information.

Bibliography

André, P., Bertrand, R. and Clement, M. (1976), "La maison à pignon en apside," *Archéologia*, no. 97, pp 28-36.

Austin, D. (1985), "Dartmoor and the Upland Village of the South-West of England," *Medieval Villages* (Hooke, D., editor), Oxford Committee for Archaeology, Monograph no. 5, pp 71-79.

Bans, J-C. and Bans, P. (1979), "Notes on the cruck-truss in Limousin," *Vernacular Architecture*, volume 10, pp 22-29

Bardel, J.-P. (1979), "Berné: Pont Calleck, le village déserté," *Archéologie en Bretagne*, no. 20-21, pp 37-42.

Barrere, M. and Batt, M. (1990), Berrien, Le Goënidou, (Finistère), *Gallia Informations - Bretagne*, pp 19, Editions CNRS.

Batt, M. (1980), "Karhaes Vihan: un village médiéval déserté, fouilles de 1979," *Archéologie en Bretagn*e, no. 24, pp 18-42.

Batt, M. (1990), Brennilis, Karhaes Vihan, Finistère, *Gallia Informations - Bretagne*, pp 19-20. Editions CNRS.

Beresford,G, (1979), "Three deserted medieval settlements on Dartmoor: A report on the late E. Marie Minters Excavations", *Medieval Archaeology*, XXIII, pp 98-158.

Beresford, M.and Hurst, J. (1971), *Deserted Medieval Villages*, Lutterworth Press, Guildford and London.

Bertrand, R.and Lucas, M.(1975), "Un village côtier du XIIéme siécle en Bretagne: Pen-er-Malo en Guidel Morbihan," *Archéologie Médievale*, 5, pp 73-101.

Burns, R.and Batt, M. (1990), "Un habitat cötier du XIIe siécle, Le Port aux Malades, Guernesey, Iles Anglo-Normandes", *Revue Archéologique de l'Ouest*, no. 7, pp 111-114.

Chapelot, J. and Fossier, R.(1980), *La Maison et le Village au Moyen Age*, Hachette, Paris.

Conte, P. (1988), "La Grange de Cournille, Saint Cerrin-de-Larche" Correze. Gallia informations-Limousin, p 173, *Editions CNRS*

Conte, P. (1990), "Le Bois des Brigands, Valiergues - un hameau medieval deserte" *Travaux d,archeologie Limousine*, Vol 10 p 130

Dedet, B. (1990), "Une maison à apsides sur l'Oppidum, de Gailhan (Gard) au milieu du Ve siécle avant J.-C. La question du plan apsidal en Gaule du sud", *GALLIA*, no. 47, pp 29-55, Editions CNRS.

Du Chatellier, P. (1907), *Les Epoques Prehistoriques et Gauloises dans le Finistère*, 2nd edition, Rennes/Quimper.

Gady, S. (1993), La Forêt de Cousage, Chasteaux, Correze Bilan Solentifique Regonal-Limousin 1992, *Service Régional de l'Archeologie ou Limousin*, pp19-20

Gasco, Y. (1983), "Une cabane médiévale au Serre de la Conque, Commune de Saint Martin-de-Londres, Herault," *Archéologie du Midi-Médiéval*, volume 1, pp 5-10.

Giot, P. R. (1982), "Enez Guennoc ou Geignoc, un ancien Microcosme Celtique," *Mélanges d'Archéologie et d'Histoire Médiévales en honneur du Doyen Michel DE BOUARD*, pp 17-180, Mémoires et Documents publié par la Société des Chartes.

Jope, E. M. and Threlfall, R. I. (1958), "Excavation of a Medieval Settlement at Beere, North Tawton, Devon," *Medieval Archaeology*, II, pp 112-140.

Le Boulanger, F., Provost, A. and Leroux, G. (1992), "Un village Carolingien sur la déviation de RN 137 à la Cocherais en Tinteniac (Ille-et-Vilaine)," *Les Dossiers du Centre Régional d'Archéologie d'Alet*, no. 20, pp 87-117.

Meirion-Jones, G. l. (1973), "The longhouse in Brittany: a provisional assessment." *Post-Medieval Archaeology*, 7, pp 1-19.

Menez, Y. and Batt, M. (1988), "L'habitat du haut moyen-age de Creac'h Gwen à Quimper Finistère," *Revue Archéologique de l'Ouest*, no. 5, pp 123-140.

Tinevez, J.-Y. and Pennec, S. (1985), *Fouilles Archéologiques de sauvetage urget à la Salverte et Melennec, Ergué-Gaberic Finistère*, Rapport de fouilles, Service Régional de l'Archéologie de Bretagne.

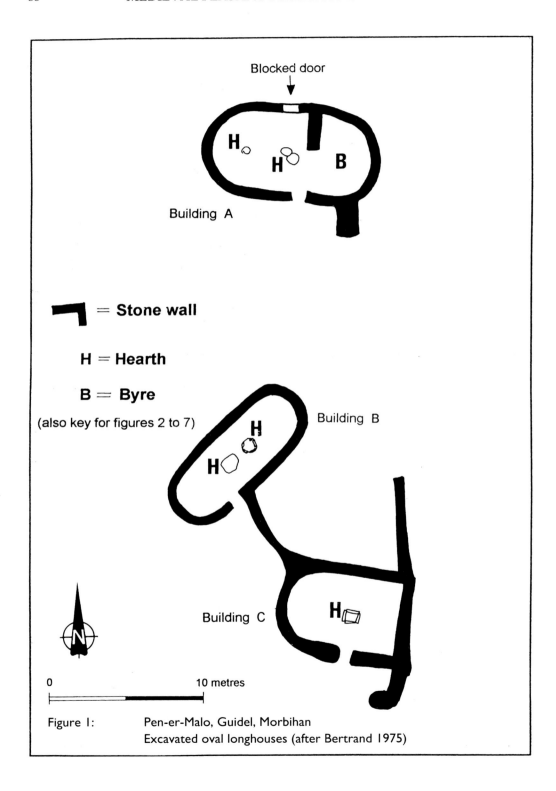

Figure 1:   Pen-er-Malo, Guidel, Morbihan
                 Excavated oval longhouses (after Bertrand 1975)

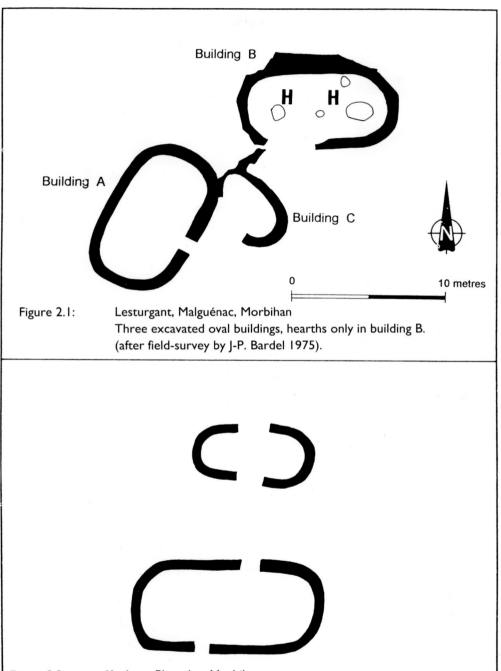

Figure 2.1: Lesturgant, Malguénac, Morbihan
Three excavated oval buildings, hearths only in building B.
(after field-survey by J-P. Bardel 1975).

Figure 2.2: Kerlano, Plumelec, Morbihan
Two excavated oval buildings, no central hearths identified
(after André 1976.)

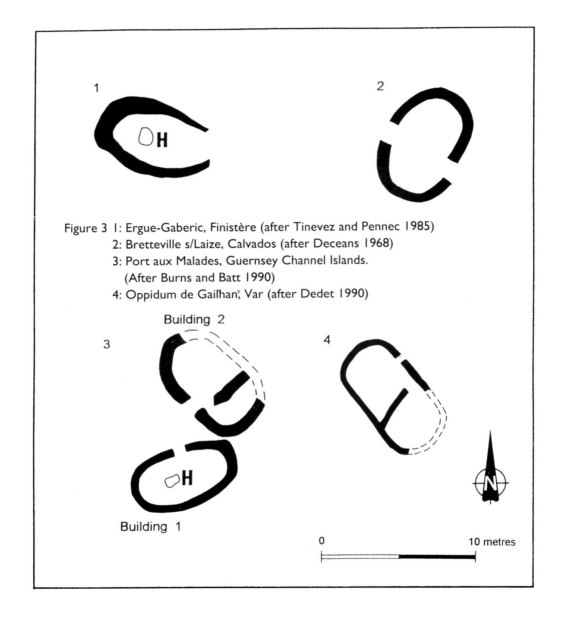

Figure 3 1: Ergue-Gaberic, Finistère (after Tinevez and Pennec 1985)
2: Bretteville s/Laize, Calvados (after Deceans 1968)
3: Port aux Malades, Guernsey Channel Islands.
(After Burns and Batt 1990)
4: Oppidum de Gailhan, Var (after Dedet 1990)

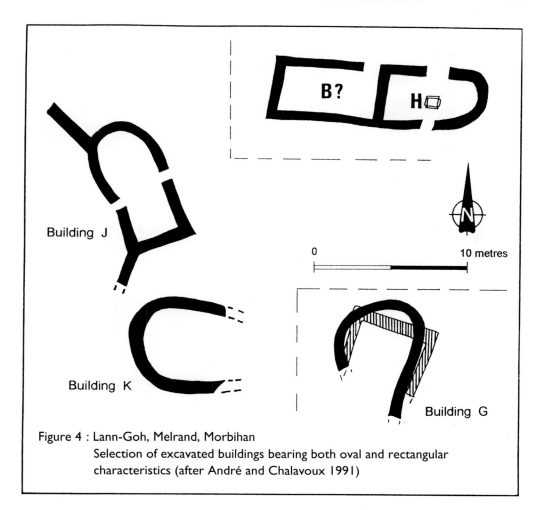

Figure 4 : Lann-Goh, Melrand, Morbihan
Selection of excavated buildings bearing both oval and rectangular
characteristics (after André and Chalavoux 1991)

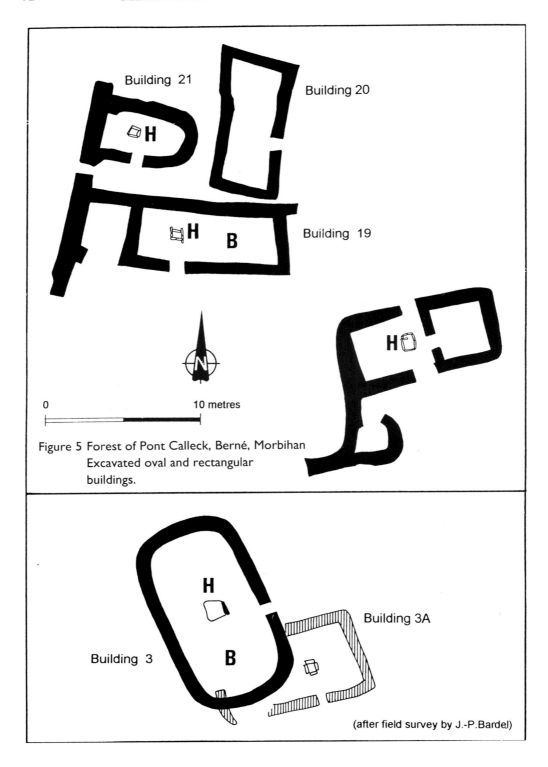

Figure 5 Forest of Pont Calleck, Berné, Morbihan
         Excavated oval and rectangular
         buildings.

(after field survey by J.-P.Bardel)

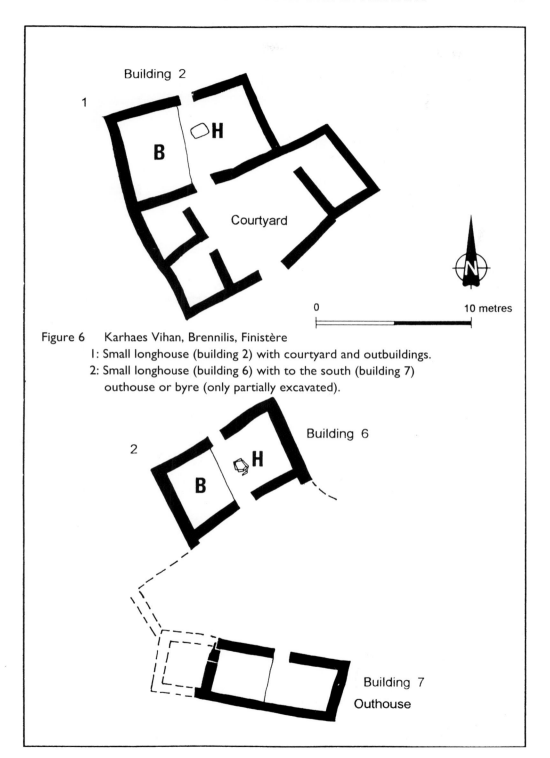

Figure 6   Karhaes Vihan, Brennilis, Finistère
          1: Small longhouse (building 2) with courtyard and outbuildings.
          2: Small longhouse (building 6) with to the south (building 7)
             outhouse or byre (only partially excavated).

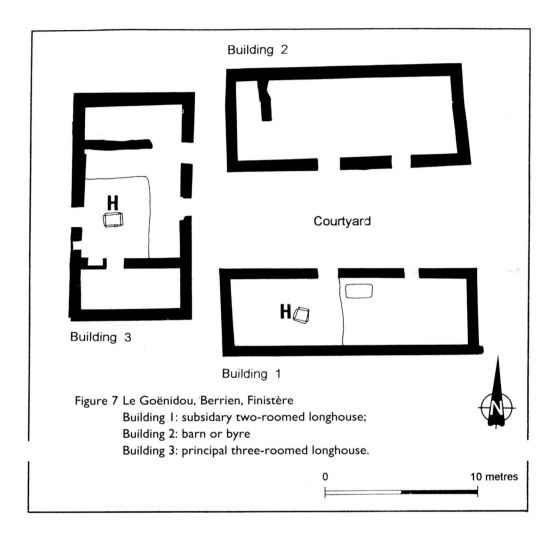

Figure 7 Le Goënidou, Berrien, Finistère
Building 1: subsidary two-roomed longhouse;
Building 2: barn or byre
Building 3: principal three-roomed longhouse.

Figure 8 Le Goënidou, Finistère
Cut-away section drawing of what a medieval longhouse
may have looked like.

Lihou Priory: A preliminary Essay [1]

BY
DARRYL M. OGIER

The Medieval monastic movement saw itself as an army of God's soldiers battling with the cohorts of Hell. Sir Richard Southern quotes a tenth-century charter which describes how abbot and monks "fight together in the strength of Christ with the sword of the spirit against the aery wiles of the devils."[2] . Ordericus Vitalis, himself a monk of Saint Evroul in Normandy, similarly advised a nobleman to "look carefully at the things which are provided for you by trained monks living in monasteries under a Rule: strenuous is the warfare which these castellans of Christ wage against the Devil[3]..." Ideas like these accounted for the foundation of some abbeys and priories in out of the way places, where the Church identified surviving pagan practices with the Devil and regarded pre-Christian remains as his work.

The same reasons may explain the location of the Priory of Sainte Marie de Lihou (otherwise Notre Dame de Lihou) on the tidal island of Lihou, off Guernsey's west coast. On the mainland opposite the island, L'Erée headland is the site of an extensive Bronze Age settlement which also shows evidence of Iron Age occupation.[4] There are indications of domestic buildings there, and, significantly, a passage grave of c. 3000-2500 BC, with signs of use c. 2000-1800 BC.[5]

The headland retained a pagan reputation in Medieval times. This is clear from the *livre de perchage* of the fief de Lihou of 1504, which lists field names.[6] The most notable are shown on Map 1. The names *grosse rocque* and *rocque au sermmonier* also occurring in the *livre* (whose exact location is not now known) perhaps refer to menhirs in the area. With regard to dehusset, we are on more certain ground. This and its variants (*dehus, tuzées* etc.) give names to several megalithic sites in Guernsey, including the well known Déhus passage grave at Bordeaux, Vale.[7] The livre de perchage of 1504 mentions also the *creeulx ez faiez* (or *faez* elsewhere). This means "the fairies' cave", and refers to the passage grave at L'Erée headland, which is still known as the *Creux ès Faies*. The name reflects the widespread belief that fairies inhabited prehistoric structures.[8]

Thus place names at L'Erée preserve memories of its pre-Christian community and their monuments. Such a superstitious reputation might account for the foundation of the Priory on Lihou, opposite the headland.[9] The Benedictine house of "castellans of Christ" there - a dependency of the great Abbey of Mont Saint Michel - may have been established in response to the district's pagan associations.[10] Indeed, the island itself may have had a sinister reputation, although proof of this is lacking.

There is no evidence of a monastic presence at Lihou before the twelfth century. Mont Saint Michel held the western half of Guernsey, probably including Lihou, for a few years after 1030, but this was lost by 1042. It had recovered part of this territory by c. 1150.[11] By the twelfth century, then, the Abbey had a long-standing association with the Lihou district. The first mention of the actual possession of Lihou by Mont Saint Michel and the existence of a church there occurs in a bull of Pope Adrian IV dated 13 February 1156.[12] By this the Pope confirmed the Abbey's enjoyment of, inter alia, a quarter of the island of Guernsey, four of its churches, two chapels, the island of Jethou, and *ecclesiam Sancte Marie de Lishou*. Robert de Torigni (Abbot of Mont Saint Michel 1154-86) came to Guernsey in 1156, and Professor and Mrs Le Patourel suggested that the Priory church may have been built in connection with his visit.[13] This remains an attractive hypothesis. The quality of the masonry suits the proposition, and the dedication to the Virgin fits well with the development of her cult in this era.

Notwithstanding this early symptom of a conventual character, it seems (in common with several other French-owned establishments in Guernsey) that later Lihou's principal function was that of a "dative" priory.[14] This type was dedicated to the collection of revenues owed to the mother house. Typically staffed by a monk or two, one being the prior, they were hardly grandiose establishments. Lihou's dative character is suggested by the fact that when in 1302 one of its monks, John de l'Espine, was murdered by John le Roer, the servant of the Prior Nicholas Baddes, only two monks appear to have been resident at the Priory.[16]

The property administered by the monks of Lihou included the fief of Notre Dame de Lihou, which is recorded as having an area of 140 vergées (fifty-six English acres) in 1331.[17] Like Lihou Priory, it was held by Mont Saint Michel, and presumably its revenues were of importance to the Priory. The Abbey's fief included a fishery called the Rousse Mare, in Guernsey, opposite Lihou (see Map 2).[18] Presumably the pond supplied the prior's table and perhaps provided revenues for the Priory as well. Mont Saint Michel's right to receive wreck from the shores around Lihou must also have involved the prior in some duties and perhaps a share of the rewards.[19]

As a priory owned by an abbey which was outside the jurisdiction of the King of England, Lihou fell into that class known to historians as the "Alien Priories". There was quite a tradition of taking those in England (mostly Norman) "into the king's hand" in times of war. This meant that the king took control, made spiritual appointments, and enjoyed priory revenues. Lihou was temporarily confiscated in this manner after the murder of 1302, but this was in common with Alien Priories in England at the time.[20] In 1337 in similar circumstances the Crown granted protection to the Prior of *Lyos* during pleasure.[21]

These actions, taken with other factors, may have meant that the fourteenth century was particularly hard for Lihou Priory, as it was for much of Europe, in a period of agrarian and epidemic crisis.[22] In 1347, whilst specifically stating that Lihou Priory was not a dependency of Saint Michel du Valle, its sister priory in Guernsey, the Crown's representative in the island noted that the fifteen *livres tournois* paid by the Priory of Saint Michel du Valle to Lihou was an inadequate stipend for the latter's prior.[23] On one occasion, in 1306, we even find a payment in the other direction, when Lihou paid twenty-one *sous* to the larger priory.[24]

The tendency of the Crown to confiscate the Alien Priories in times of war culminated in an Act of Parliament of 1414 which permanently vested all English possessions of foreign religious houses in the Crown. The holdings of French establishments in Guernsey fell within the act's ambit. There is a hint, however, that some ecclesiastical properties in Guernsey were confiscated before the act's promulgation. A letter apparently of 1405 written from Guernsey to the Lords of Henry IV's Council refers to the ruin into which the Priory of Saint Michel du Valle had fallen by that time.[25] This suggests that Lihou may also have been abandoned by Mont Saint Michel before the act of 1414.[26]

Nonetheless, throughout the fifteenth century, although the living of Lihou fell into the gift of the English power rather than the French abbot, Mont Saint Michel continued to act as if it still possessed the Priory. This matched the policy of other Norman houses which had been deprived of their English interests.[27] Presumably the Abbey hoped for the recovery of Lihou and a resumption of the status quo, as had been the case with earlier confiscations. Thus in 1448 the Abbot of Mont Saint Michel wrote to the Prior of Lihou, who although unnamed was presumably a recent English appointee, seeking his attendance at the Abbey to present valid letters of office.[28] This tenacity is similarly seen in that an appointment as Prior of Lihou was held at Mont Saint Michel as late as 1523, in which year Jacques Tournier, a monk of the Abbey, formally resigned the office. It is unlikely that he actually enjoyed the Priory or its revenues.[29]

The reversion of the interest in Lihou Priory of the Duke of Gloucester as *Seigneur des Iles* 1435-46[30] was purportedly given by Henry VI to Eton College in 1444.[31] However, the Priory seems to have remained in the hands (and gift) of Gloucester and the success or to the estates before reverting to the Crown in 1487, when the Countess of Warwick surrendered her rights in the Islands to Henry VII.[32]

In 1500, Henry in turn granted the Priory to Dr Ralf Leonard, a Dominican friar.[33] Although clearly a man of education and rank, Leonard appears not to have been an absentee, living in England, but to have resided in Guernsey, although probably not on Lihou itself. This is suggested in the records of the court of fief Saint Michel, which note his appearance before it pursuing an action on 20 June 1510.[34] A document dated 1519 at Saint Peter Port Church refers to a house in Fountain Street "where the Prior of Lihou lives" (*la meson ou le Prieur de Lihou demeuroit*).[35] It is likely that this was the house Leonard inhabited. Certainly an urban life would have been better suited to the avowed role of a Dominican than existence on a tidal island, where opportunities for evangelism and learning would have been few, to say the least.

The grants to Leonard of the office of prior and subsequent appointments show that notwithstanding the removal of the French interest, Lihou Priory remained a religious establishment, although under the supervision of the

English Crown rather than a Norman abbey. This was characteristic of the fate of the Alien Priories in England too, where the native church was in large part the beneficiary of the deprivation of its foreign counterparts.[36] In the fifteenth and early sixteenth centuries, Lihou Priory maintained this religious character, although usually referred to as a "chapel", probably indicating the absence of monks and the employment of a secular priest to celebrate masses there and administer its income. Revenues continued to be paid to it and some new ones were initiated. The *partage* of the realty of Collas Robyn of 1520 notes an annual *rente* of ten denerels of wheat due to the *Chappelle de Lyhou*.[37] A custumal of fief de Sausmarez of 1482 similarly refers to two quarters of wheat *rente* yearly owed to *La Chappelle de Notre Damme de Lihou*.[38] Lihou also had a place in the religious affiliations of private individuals. The will of Jean Girart, dated 1522, bequeathed one gros to Notre Dame de Lihou.[39] Thomas de Havilland's will of 1535 (proven 1537) leaves twelve shillings sterling to the *capelle beatae marie de Lihou*.[40]

The return submitted by the Bailiff and Governor's lieutenant of Guernsey in 1535 as part of Henry VIII's Valor Ecclesiasticus referred to the income of "Lihow" as being some five pounds sterling, together with tithes to the value of ten shillings.[41] The officers who produced the report may well have been as disingenuous as they were with other ecclesiastical interests in Guernsey.[42] Certainly they did not refer to the annual payments owed.

Small though it may have been, the income of the chapel was worth having. In the first year of Elizabeth I André Powes was referred to as warden of "Le Howe".[43] Powes was a cleric of some standing. He had been appointed rector of Saint Pierre du Bois in 1525 and Saint Martin two years later.[44] He also served as the Crown's Receiver in Guernsey in the fifteen-twenties and thirties.[45] Thomas de Beaugy, the rector of Saint Peter Port from 1556, and Saint Sampson from 1569,[46] is called the "farmer" of the fief de Lihou in 1559, and referred to as "Prior" in following years.[47] By 1562 he was called the former chaplain or farmer.[48] John After, one of the Royal Commissioners appointed in 1563, is known to have enjoyed the "Priorie callid Lehowe" during his residence in Guernsey.[49] By 1572 another minister, François Regnault, who is recorded as vicar at Saint Pierre du Bois in the same year,[50] was said to be a former farmer of the island.[51]

There is some evidence that by the fifteen-eighties the emoluments once paid to the Priory went to the Diocese of Winchester, of which Guernsey formed part from the late fifteen-sixties.[52] However, as with much other ecclesiastical property in Guernsey and elsewhere in this period, the revenues of the Priory were soon secularised. On 30 July 1586 Lihou Island was granted by the Crown to Thomas Wigmore, Bailiff of Guernsey 1581-87.[53] Wigmore in turn surrendered his interest to his uncle Sir Thomas Leighton (Governor of Guernsey 1570-1610) on 19 December 1596.[54]

Peter Heylyn described "Lehu" in 1629, saying that it was ... appertaining once unto the Dean, but now unto the Governour. Famous for a little oratory or

Chantery there once erected and dedicated to the honour of the Virgin Mary, who by the people in those times, was much sued to by the name of our Lady of Lehu. A place long since demolished in the ruin of it ... but now the ruines of it are scarce visible, there being almost nothing left of it but the steeple, which serveth only as a sea-marke, and to which as any of that party sail along, they strike their top sail. ... such a religious opinion they have of the place, that though the Saint be gone, the wals yet shall still be honoured.[55]

Given the Priory's recent acquisition by the States of Guernsey, its archeological significance, and the occasion for this publication, Heylyn's last few words make an appropriate and optimistic conclusion.

Notes

1   I was first asked to look at the history of Lihou Priory by Bob Burns, and it is appropriate that this essay should appear in his *festschrift*; the more so since it has the character of that archaeological beast, the "interim report": no doubt substantial modifications to Lihou's history will be needed once the investigations initiated by Bob Burns and Ken Barton progress, and historical researches advance. Where necessary dates have been adjusted to a year beginning 1 January.

2   Quoted by R. W. Southern, *Western Society and the Church in the Middle Ages* (Harmondsworth, 1970) pp. 224-25.

3   Quoted, *Ibid*. p 225.

4   Heather Sebire, personal communication.

5   I. Kinnes and J. A. Grant, *Les Fouaillages and the Megalithic Monuments of Guernsey* (Alderney, 1983) pp. 44-5.

6   *Livre de perchage* of *Franc Fieu de Nostre Dame de Lihou*, 1504, copy of Island Archive Service (hereafter "Island Archives") collated with map showing current field names of States Cadastre, Guernsey. The origin of the *Livre de perchage* of fief de Lihou, 1504 is in the uncatalogued MSS of fief le Comte, Greffe, Guernsey.

7   Kinnes and Grant, *Les Fouaillages*, pp. 53-55.

8   K. V. Thomas, *Religion and the Decline of Magic; studies in popular beliefs in sixteenth and seventh century England* (Harmondsworth, 1975) p. 728; K. Briggs, *The Fairies in English Literature and Tradition* (London, 1967) p. 107.

9   cf. G. Daniel, *Megaliths in History* (London, 1972) p. 59: which concluded it is "difficult to envisage why there should be a Christian occupation of some megalithic sites, unless a real tradition of their importance as special and sacred places was carried through the period of the Bronze and Early Iron Age of barbarian Europe and into historic times." *Ibid* pp. 27-32 quotes several examples of churches built upon or incorporating megalithic tombs, with the intention of Christianising them. For examples of the Christianisation of pagan sites in Guernsey see J. McCormack, *Channel Island Churches* (Chichester, 1986) especially pp. 133, 146; and for Breton parallels L. Grinsell, "The Christianisation of prehistoric and other pagan sites", *Landscape History* viii (1986) pp.30-31.

10   The same *rationale* might account for the presence of a wayside cross - the *croes de Lihou* - on the headland (*Livre de Perchage, 1504*). Mr Lenfestey (personal communication) points out that it may have been significant that the cross overlooked both the *dehusset* and the *creeulx ez faiez*. The *camp varouf* probably refers not directly to a werewolf (Norman French *varou*) but to the Varouf or Variouf family which lived in Guernsey in the Middle Ages.

11   A. H. Ewen, 'The Fiefs of the Island of Guernsey,' *Transactions of La Société Guernesiaise* (until 1922 called the Guernsey Society of Natural Science and Local Research, and hereafter TSG) vol xvii p 177.

12   *Cartulaire des Iles Normandes* pp. 15-19, dated by J.H. Round, *Calendar of Documents Preserved in France* (London, 1899) pp. 268-69. These speculations do not preclude other factors influencing the choice of site. The Priory may even have been a refoundation of an earlier establishment. Certainly other places in the Channel Islands already had Christian associations in the Celtic era. The maritime environment and isolation of Lihou would have appealed to *peregrini* as much as it may have done to some more ascetically inclined members of the Benedictine Order. Richard Morris states that 'islands which were cut off from the mainland at high tide but accessible at low water seem to have held a special attraction' to the early monastic movement (R. Morris, *Churches in the Landscape* [London, 1989] p. 110). The conjectured date of the foundation of Lihou's church (see below) accords well with the Gallican recolonisation of eremetic sites in the area in the twelfth century: L. Musset, "Essai sur l'ancien monachisme insulaire autour des côtes du Cotentin et de l'Avranchin": in *Nédélèqueries: recueil d'articles offerts à Yves Nédélec archiviste départmental de la Manche de 1954 à 1994* (Saint-Lô, 1994) , p. 366.

13   *Cartulaire des Iles Normandes* pp. 239-42; *Chronica: the chronicle of Robert de Torigni, Abbot of the Monastery of St Michael -in-Peril-of-the-Sea* in R. Howlett (ed.), *Chronicles of the Reigns of Stephen, Henry II, and Richard I* (4 vols, Rolls Series, 1885-89) iv pp. 335-37; J. and J. Le Patourel, "Lihou Priory: excavations 1952" *TSG* vol xv p. 180. See also the reference to Professor Musset's article in the previous note.

14   On the dative priories of the Channel Islands see W. Stevenson, "English rule in the Channel Islands in a period of transition 1204-1259" *TSG* Vol xx pp. 237-40. The Prior of Lihou in 1270 was one Pierre Bernard: *Cartulaire des Iles Normandes* p. 179.

15   C. Platt, *The Abbeys and Priories of Medieval England* (London, 1984) p. 174.

16   J.H. Le Patourel, "The murder on Lihou Island in 1302" *The Quarterly Review of the Guernsey Society* vii (1951) pp. 3-6.

17   H. de Sausmarez (ed.), *The Extentes of Guernsey 1248   and 1331: and other documents relating to ancient usages and customs in that island* (Guernsey, 1934) p. 83.

18   I am grateful to Mr Lenfestey for supplying details of the extent of the Rousse Mare. The *livre de perchage* of 1504 records its area as thirty-nine *vergées* (15.6 English acres).

19   *Cartulaire des Iles Normandes* pp. 26-30, 33-34, 45-46, 172, 239, 224; *Calendar of Patent Rolls 1272-81* (London, 1901) p. 435; *Rolls of the Assizes held in the Channel Islands in the second year of the reign of King Edward II A.D. 1309* (Jersey, 1903) pp. 22, 41-44, 47, 128, 141.

20   Platt, *The Abbeys and Priories of Medieval England* , p. 173.

21   *Calendar of Patent Rolls 1334-38* (London, 1895) p. 492. cf. M.M. Morgan, "The Suppression of the Alien Priories" *History* xxvi (1941-42) p. 205.

22   The Channel Islands were severely affected by the Black Death: P. Zeigler, *The Black Death* (London, 1969) p. 125.

23   *Cartulaire des Iles Normandes* p. 201. This annuity is also attested in 1314 and 1359: *Cartulaire des Iles Normandes* p. 172; Island Archives: *Records and Documents* (MS volumes ex Bailiff's Office) iii p. 229.

24   Island Archives: copy of rolls of Vale Priory no. 3 as cited in *Cartulaire des Iles Normandes* p. 435. Mont Saint Michel's late thirteenth-century chantry records referred to two *sous tournois* payable by Lihou to the Abbey . The Vale Priory owed six: *Cartulaire des Iles Normandes* pp. 45-46.

25   H. Nicolas (ed.), *Proceedings and Ordinances of the Privy Council of England* ii (London, 1834) pp. 106-07.

26   This was not without English precedent: Morgan, *"The Suppression of the Alien Priories"* p. 207.

27   Platt, *The Abbeys and Priories of Medieval England*, p. 177.

28   *Cartulaire des Iles Normandes* pp. 218-9.

29   *Cartulaire des Iles Normandes* p 219.

30   T.W.M. de Guérin, "Our Hereditary Governors" *TSG* vol vi p. 221.

31   *Calendar of Patent Rolls 1441-46* (London, 1905) p236. In connection with this paragraph I gratefully acknowledge the assistance of Ian Hart of the Royal Commission on Historical Manuscripts and Penny Hatfield, the archivist at Eton College.

32   De Guérin, "Our Hereditary Governors" p. 226.

33   T. Rymer (ed.), *Foedera* (20 vols, London 1727-35) xii (1727) p. 747.

34   Greffe: MS registers of fief Saint Michel, i, f. 9v, to be located by J. Le Patourel *et al* (eds), *List of Documents in the Greffe , Guernsey* vol. i (List & Index Society Special Series vol. 2, London, 1969) p. 76.

35   Greffe: copy in Lee MSS, ii p. 164 to be located by Le Patourel *et al* (eds), *List of Documents in the Greffe, Guernsey* vol. i p. 87.

36   Morgan, *"The Suppression of the Alien Priories"* pp. 207, 210.

37   Greffe, *lettre sous sceau*, to be located by J.H. Lenfestey (ed.), *List of Documents in the Greffe, Guernsey volume 3. Greffe Collection: records under sign manual, signature or seal (other than the Bailiwick Seal)* (Guernsey, 1983) p. 107, item 2.

38   Greffe, *lettre sous sceau* to be located by J.H. Lenfestey (ed.), *List of Documents in the Greffe, Guernsey volume ii: documents under Bailiwick Seal* (List & Index Society Special Series vol. 11, London, 1978) p. 105, item 61. There is another copy at Island Archives: uncatalogued Guille papers, auctioneer's ref. no. 51.

39   Greffe, Girart MS p. 3 to be located by Le Patourel *et al* (eds), *List of Documents in the Greffe, Guernsey* p. 52.

40   Greffe, transcripts of wills in uncatalogued MSS of Sir Edgar MacCulloch.

41   Caley, J. & Hunter, J. (eds), *Valor Ecclesiasticus, temp. Henrici VIII, auctoritate regia institutus* (6 vols, London, 1810–34) ii p. 27.

42   D.M. Ogier, *Reformation and Society in Guernsey* (Woodbridge, 1996) ch. 3.

43   *Exchequer Ancient Deeds - DD Series 1101-1645 (E211)* (List and Index Society, vol. 200, London,1993) p. 293.

44   G.E. Lee (ed.), "Extraits des Registres du Secrètariat de l'Évêché de Coutances 1487–1557" *Bulletin of Société Jersiaise* xiv (1889) pp. 443, 444.

45   D.M. Ogier, "Reformation and Society in Guernsey , *c.* 1500 - *c.* 1640" (University of Warwick PhD thesis, 2 vols, 1993) i p. 50.

46   Lee (ed.), "Extraits des Registres du Secrètariat de l'Évêché de Coutances 1487–1557" p. 453; G.E. Lee (ed.), "Winchester Registers" *Guernsey Magazine* February 1890; de Beaugy was referred to as a *cure* at S. Michel du Valle, in 1572: R. MacCulloch (ed.), *Recueil d'Ordonnances de la Cour Royale de Guernesey* i,1533–1800 (Guernsey, 1852) p. 30.

47   Island Archives: *Records and Documents* (MS volumes ex Bailiff's Office) iii p. 20; Greffe, *Vers en Meubles* i, f. 144v, ii ff. 85r, 85v, iii ff. 128r, 129r, 130v, 131v, 132r, to be located by Le Patourel *et al* (eds), *List of Documents in the Greffe, Guernsey* vol. i , p. 32.

48   Island Archives: *Records and Documents* (MS volumes ex Bailiff's Office) ii, p. 91.

49   British Library, Lansdowne MS cxi art. 50 f. 124.

50   MacCulloch (ed.), *Recueil d'Ordonnances de la Cour Royale de Guernesey* i p. 30.

51   Island Archives: *Records and Documents* (MS volumes ex Bailiff's Office) iii p. 98.

52   Island Archives: *Records and Documents* (MS volumes ex Bailiff's Office) v p. 14.

53   *List of Documents in the Greffe, Guernsey volume 3* p. 9.

54   The document effecting this was cited in Court proceedings in Guernsey in the 1980s in *Constables of S. Pierre du Bois -v- Wootton*. I have seen a photocopy

in private hands. Unfortunately the whereabouts of the original (which is in English, in English form) are now unknown.

55   P. Heylyn, *A Full Relation of two Journeys: The One Into the Main–Land of France, the Other Into some of the adjacent Islands* (London, 1656) p. 298

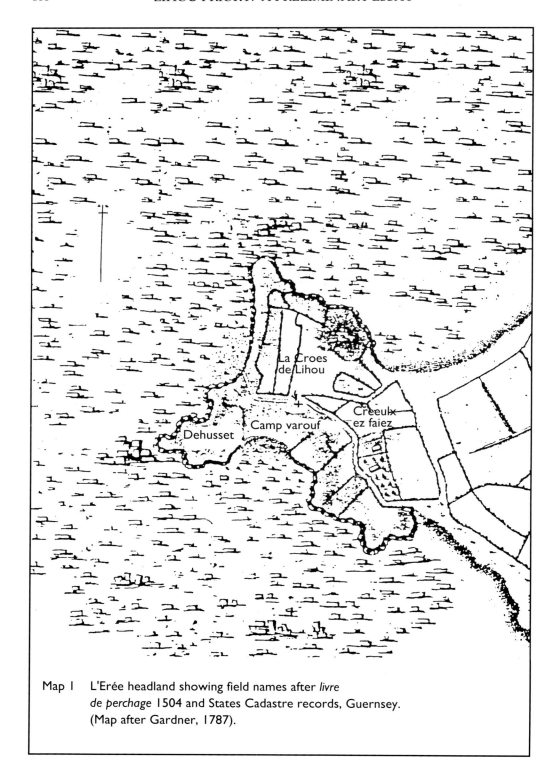

Map 1   L'Erée headland showing field names after *livre de perchage* 1504 and States Cadastre records, Guernsey. (Map after Gardner, 1787).

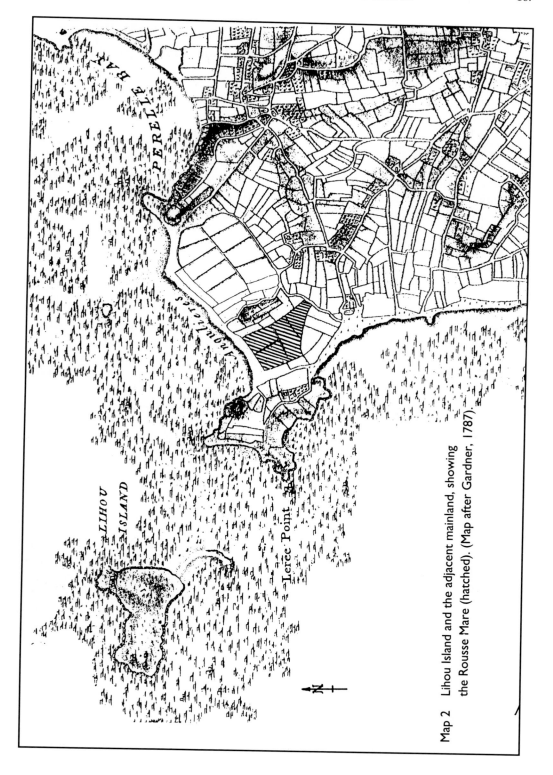

Map 2   Lihou Island and the adjacent mainland, showing the Rousse Mare (hatched). (Map after Gardner, 1787).

A Group of Normandy Stonewares
of the Second Half of the 15th Century, Hamptonne Farm, Jersey

BY
MARGARET B. FINLAISON

This small offering is to a friend and advisor. It has been my good fortune that our collaboration has also been close friendship, from the start in the early 1970s when our efforts at rescue work had yet to stir awareness in the Islands, through to the easier times of today. No-one has done more to illuminate the archaeology of Guernsey than Bob Burns, and his quite outstanding success has been due to a considerable natural talent, a capacity for very hard work and the gift of a generous personality. Guernsey has indeed been fortunate in its officer. I hope he will forgive me for returning here to that subject from which neither of us have ever been able to completely escape . . . Normandy stoneware.

This is a preliminary report on part of a midden deposit and is confined to the Normandy stonewares. During the archaeological examination of the group of farm buildings destined to become the Jersey Museum of Rural Life, the project director, Dr Warwick Rodwell cut a section through a small clay quarry. This pit had been dug to provide material for the construction of the main farm building. The writer undertook to excavate the rest of the pit which appeared, from its unweathered base, to have become a receptacle for household rubbish soon after the house was occupied.

There is no documentary evidence for the construction of Hamptonne house, but it is known to have been occupied in the 16th century and permission is recorded in 1445 for the building of a Colombier. This date would not conflict with that of the first deposits in the midden.

Bob Burns has recently written a comprehensive history and description of Normandy stoneware as it relates to the islands[1], and repeating those descriptions here seems to be unnecessary. Both the Domfront and Bessin types in this pit were accompanied throughout by the so-called Pink/Grey or Buffwares. These are hard smooth earthenwares most often with a grey core, while the early forms can be noticeably gritted with quartz grains. In Jersey, that with buff or the scarcer pink/grey (reduced) colour occurs on all sites of this period, sometimes in quantity which suggests there may be a production site of some size. It seems likely in the end that it will prove to be in the vicinity of Beauvais or Martincamp. At the moment, Buffware first seems to appear in Jersey not long before 1450. Both Normandy stoneware and Buffware forms can be identical.

The Lower deposits. Mid-late 15th century (Nos. 1 - 19)
These comprise Domfront wares (1-11) and Bessin wares (12-19).

They were lying directly in or on the clay at the base of the quarry with unweathered chips of granite from mason's work and fragments of roof slate. The accompanying pottery included Developed Normandy Gritty ware, Chocolate Brown ware, Buffware, a grey stoneware jug probably from Beauvais, and a lobed cup. A jetton depicting a mounted knight has not yet been identified.

Domfront wares. (Nos. 1-11)

No. 1 is a jug with neck cordon of horizontal cornice type, one of several jugs. These have been illustrated by Bob Burns[2] and from excavations at Caen[2]. In both instances they are considered to be 15th century. The Caen vessel shows a body decoration of vertical applied bands which are also found here (Nos. 6 and 7).

The jugs Nos. 4 and 5 have salmon fabric and surfaces with a high, metallic grey sheen. Nos. 8 and 9 have surfaces of a uniform dull, matt grey overall. No. 10 represents one of a number of ridged strap handles. The gritted grey-brown fabric and rim form of No.11 resembles examples of early Domfront from the excavation of the Ecrehous Priory[4], where the bodies of the vessels are rilled.

Bessin wares (Nos. 12-19)

With the exception of Nos. 12 and 13, all these have external surfaces heavily blotched with rough, matt, grey reduction.

The Upper deposits. Late l5th-Early 16th century. (Nos. 20 - 33)

This was a homogenous fill. The associated wares included Developed Normandy Grittyware (a little), Chocolate Brown ware, Buffware including a footed jug with internal green glaze, a gritted and green glazed Normandy chafing dish, a small N W French jar with white fabric and green glaze, Iberian coarseware body sherds and German stoneware. They are all Bessin ware. No Domfront was present.

The fragment of vertical, applied banding, No. 20, is a Bessin example of this decoration. The jugs Nos. 21-23 are of a form generally dated later but these were well within the fill. No.25 is a jug of a type which occurred lower in the deposits. Red stoneware or the 'Redwares' considered by Kenneth Barton[5] to be 15th century are represented here by the chafing dish No.28 and handle No.29. No.30 is a jug with flat neck band. Two of four costrel spouts are illustrated, Nos.32 and 33.

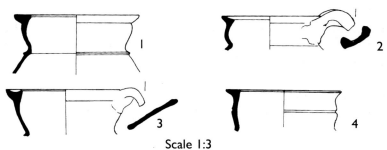

Scale 1:3

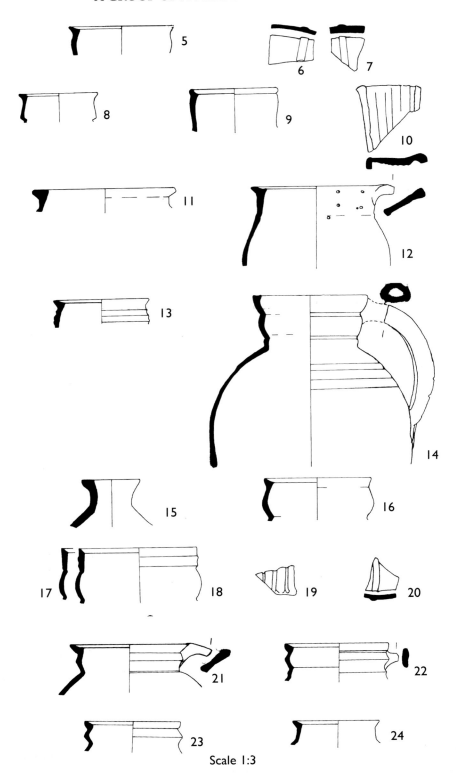

Scale 1:3

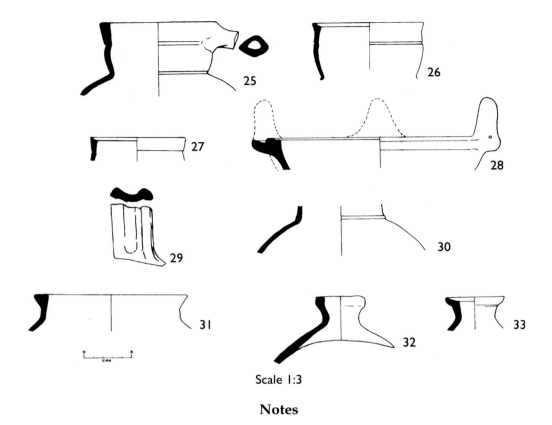

Scale 1:3

Notes

1.   Burns, R., 1991. 'Post-Medieval Normandy Stonewares from Guernsey,' in *Custom and Ceramics Essays* presented to Kenneth Barton. Wickham, pp 104-112.

2.   Burns, R., op. cit. pp 111-112.

3.   Marin, J. Y., Berteaux J. J., *et al.*, 1988. 'L'ancien quartier Saint Pierre de Caen - fouilles de parking du Château 1986.' *Musee de Normandie. Caen*, No.7, p 34.

4.   Report in publication.

5.   Examples of these are illustrated in: Barton, K.J., 1977, 'Medieval and post medieval pottery from Gorey Castle.' *Bulletin Société Jersiaise*, XXII, pp 69-82.

Acknowledgement

I am grateful to Warwick Rodwell for allowing this to be published in advance of the main Hamptonne research report.

Coupée Lane : The Glass

An Initial Observation

BY

VIVIEN FERNEYHOUGH

Introduction

Coupée Lane forms one side of a triangular area of land which is completed by Cornet Street and Cliff Street in the parish of St. Peter Port, Guernsey. It is situated on high ground to the south of the town centre (See St. Peter Port Map). Documentary evidence reveals that from the medieval period onwards this part of St. Peter Port, with its relative ease of access to the commercial area of town which centered around the Town Church ("ecclesia Sancti Petri de Portu") and the port itself, was fairly well developed (Le Patourel, 1933-36).

La Tour Beauregard (c.1350) was built about 50 metres to the north of what is now Coupée Lane. This tower, along with la Tour Gand situated to the north of the town, formed part of a defensive scheme which had been built by order of Edward III due to repeated French raids during this period of the Hundred Years War and after the destruction of Jerbourg Castle which had been the previous place of refuge (Cox 1905-08, pp.337-338). Both of these towers have since been demolished.

There is also evidence to suggest that in the 13th and 14th centuries close trading links had developed between Guernsey and Gascony resulting in a strong mercantile element in Guernsey society (Le Patourel 1933-36, pp.183-184). The Lombards were reputed to have lived in the Cornet Street area and indeed Edith Carey mentions that Lombardy House was used as a counting house in the 19th century. Moreover, the area with which this paper is concerned still had a strong merchant presence at this time (Carey 1933-36, p.154).

The historical evidence therefore suggested that this site would be rewarding from an archaeological perspective. Furthermore, three excavations had previously taken place in the vicinity of the church of St. Barnabas (which is in close proximity to the possible site of La Tour Beauregard). These excavations have provided evidence of the town ditch in the Cliff Street - Coupée Lane locale. In 1982 a completely enclosed area of land which had been lying waste behind a partly derelict house fronting onto Cornet Street became available for excavation. Three trenches were dug, and the full site report will give details of the contents excavated. However the site proved to be rich in artefacts and what follows is a discussion of representative examples of the glass finds.

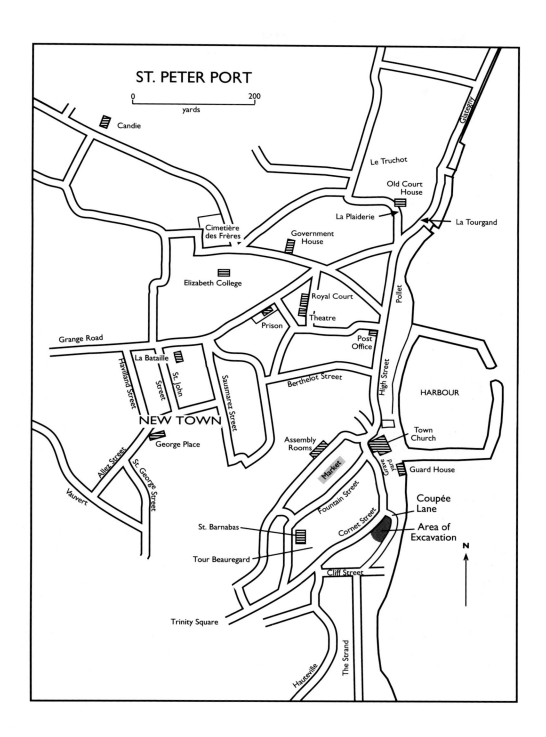

ST. PETER PORT

The Glass

A total of 842 fragments of glass were recovered from this site. They range in date from medieval to modern with an emphasis on the 18th and 19th centuries. Three typological groups are represented:- Vessel Glass (66 fragments), Bottle Glass (419 fragments) and Window Glass (347 fragments). The assemblage also contained 2 glass beads, 5 fragments of utility glass, 22 lead cames and 3 unidentified fragments.

Given the history of the site, there was very little 12th - 14th century material and first indications of artefacts being in a secure level do not occur on the site until 1450 - 1480. However, one trench revealed large truncated pits cut into an orange/yellow clay - identical to that used for mortar in medieval buildings. Therefore it is believed that the site was exploited for its clay from c. 1400 - 1450 and that most traces of occupation before then would have been removed. Nevertheless, three examples of medieval glass were recovered and sent to John Shepherd at the Museum of London for verification. It is important to stress the fragmentary nature of these examples, due in part to the nature of the site outlined above and also due to the instability of medieval potash glass (Charleston 1984, p. 258). Factors such as these make positive identification difficult. Fig 1:1 is possibly a fragment from the body of a small flask or phial. The glass has weathered to a dark brown colour due to the effects of prolonged burial. The ribbed decoration has been made by optic blowing, which means that a gather of molten glass (the paraison) is inflated into a highly ribbed mould and then further inflated outside of the mould. The fragment is thought to be of a type similar to flasks nos. 220-1, the gourds nos. 238-9 and the bottle no. 241 (Rouen Catalogue 1989 - 1990, pp. 240, 249, 250-51) and dated to the 14th century. Examples of these types have been found in the Languedoc, Nimes, Avignon and Besançon regions in France.

A fragment of colourless glass (not illustrated) was also found but was so small that a tentative identification has to be made. It appears to be a fragment from the lower part of the bowl of a goblet - possibly from a "verre a tige". This type of vessel is known in France (Foy 1989, pp.204-9, 263) and examples have also been found in Southampton, the city of London and Holland (Charleston 1975, p.205).

The medieval window glass fragments (not illustrated) came from two individual examples. One, made up of many friable bits which are virtually decomposed and the other, with surface decomposition are thought to be "broad" or "muff" glass as the friable piece shows the fire-rolled edge of this type of glass. Broad glass was formed by blowing an elongated bubble of glass, cutting off both ends and cutting the resultant cylinder (which could be up to 5 feet in length) lengthwise; after re-heating the cylinder was flattened. This method of making window glass had been used as early as c.1100 in Lorraine (Newman 1977, p.50), but these fragments should be broadly dated 12th - 16th century.

Three fragments of "cristallo" were found and came from the bodies of two different vessels. "Cristallo" is a type of soda glass developed in Venice c.1500 using pure siliceous pebbles and sea-plant ashes (barilla) or natron, with manganese as a decolourant. Glass-makers from early times had sought to produce a glass that resembled rock crystal (natural quartz) and the development of "cristallo" enabled the Venetians to dominate glassmaking for the next two and a half centuries (Charleston 1984, pp.43-5). However, in the 16th century many glass-workers migrated from Murano to most countries in Europe, thus enabling glasshouses in France and the Netherlands to produce glass "à la façon de Venise" (Charleston 1992, p.134). Indeed, by the mid 16th century "cristallo à la façon Venise" was being manufactured at the Crutched Friars glasshouse in London (Charleston 1975, p134).

Of the three fragments of "cristallo" found at the Coupée Lane site, two came from the same beaker but from different areas. One fragment came from, a large circular pit and the other was found in a layer of clay-like soil containing lumps of bright yellow clay. Both fragments are of colourless glass with a smokey brown tint and some seeding. They originally formed part of the body of a beaker that had a mould blown raised lozenge pattern on it. Possible parallels have been found in Southampton (Charleston 1975, fig. 225, no. 157) and Poole (Charleston 1992, fig.80, no. 51). The illustrated fragment (fig.2:2) could either be from a goblet bowl or a beaker body that had an applied and tooled decoration. The glass is colourless with some seeding and slight surface pitting due to burial: all three fragments can be dated mid to late 16th century. Like all of the glass discussed here the "cristallo" is an import. The exact provenance of such items of luxury consumption is difficult to ascertain due to the peripatetic nature of some of the Venetian glass-workers as cited above. However, the existence of such fine glass on this site suggests that the higher levels of Guernsey society were aware of the latest developments in glass production and reflected the contemporary taste for luxury glass.

Turning now to examples of 18th - 19th century glass. Of the two glass beads recovered one was a yellow glass annulated bead found in a 19th century deposit (not illustrated). The other bead (fig.2:3) is an elongated "baluster" shape; originally dark blue, it has dark brown surface weathering. This is probably a bugle bead used in embroidered decoration on ladies dresses. They were imported into England from Venice, although some were made at a factory established in the late 1750s near Rye (Newman 1987, p.52). Although Newman states that they were of an elongated cylindrical form, it seems reasonable to postulate that variations could have been made.

The 18th century wine glass is represented by a fragment from a domed and folded foot (fig.1:4). It is made of lead glass and is colourless with some surface decay. It was found in association with mid 18th century pottery. Charleston states that by the 18th century "English crystal was the cynosure of continental makers, and all efforts were bent to emulating it" (Charleston 1984, p.142). English glass of lead, developed by Ravenscroft in the 1670s, satisfied the demand for a " very good cleer whit[e] sound Mettall" (Charleston 1992, p.135). This was a period when wine glass bowls and stems showed great variety (Wilkinson 1968, pp.108-175). Unfortunately the incomplete foot fragment from Coupée Lane makes it difficult to identify what form the stem and bowl of this particular glass took. What it does suggest is that the merchant class in this area continued to reflect contemporary taste and demand for high quality glass.

Bottles

As mentioned earlier, 419 bottle fragments were recovered. These were predominantly wine bottles of 18th - 19th century date, together with one case bottle (base and part body) and 65 apothecaries phials (fragments and complete phials). Four modern ink bottles were also found. Of the wine bottles, four representative examples will be discussed, all of which are of well attested types. Three are of a mid 18th century date the first of which is a base and body fragment of a mould blown case bottle with open pontil mark (fig.2:5). The glass is pale green with surface decay. This type of square bottle was able to be crated and stored in cases or chests as part of a ships cargo. Although they were in use from the late 16th century onwards, the associated pottery is of a mid 18th century date. A neck and string rim fragment from a mallet bottle was recovered from a late 18th/early 19th century fill between two stub walls. This bottle type can be dated 1725-1760 (Dumbrell 1983, pp.79-86). In the same feature as the mallet bottle fragment, the neck and string rim of a small wine bottle broadly dated 1760-1800 was found (fig.1:7). The poorly tooled coil-like string rim suggests that it may be French in origin (Dumbrell 1983, pp.128-134). The final example from this group is the neck and string rim of an early 19th century cylindrical wine bottle (fig.1:8). This bottle was mould blown and the string rim construction makes it dateable to 1800-10 (Dumbrell 1983, p.93). Wine bottles of this date are representative of the period when the search for uniformity to regulate capacity (begun in England in the 1730's) produced a bottle suitable for binning.

The search for uniformity in capacity is also reflected in the changing forms of apothecaries phials. All the phials recovered from the Coupée Lane site are of a late 18th/early 19th century date. Seven complete phials and 42 out of 65 phial fragments come from a black ashy fill between the stud walls. The seven complete phials provide a representative sample of 18th - 19th century types, three of which are illustrated. The form of apothecaries phials changed little from the late 17th to the early 19th century. They were mainly cylindrical with a short neck, everted rims and a "kick" in the base. One difference was that by the early 19th century, decolourized or flint glass was being used (Charleston 1975, pp.214-215) and by the 1840s phials were moulded rather than free blown.

Fig 1:9 is a free blown cylindrical phial in pale green glass, approximately 3 fl.oz. capacity and of a late 18th century date. This phial is fairly crudely made and slightly unstable, due in part to the pontil mark being proud of the base and is illustrative of a problem that pharmacists had in the late 18th early 19th century regarding stability and accuracy of dose (Crellin and Scott, pp.148-149). Fig 2:10 is a colourless glass free blown cylindrical phial, approximately $1^1/_2$ fl.oz. capacity and similar to Type 1D in the Wellcome Collection of British glass dispensing containers (Crellin and Scott, fig.1). Figure2:11 is a pale blue/green steeple shaped phial, approximately 2 fl.oz. capacity and dateable 1800-1850. The glass has been blown into a two part mould which has resulted in seam marks across the base and vertically up to the shoulders. The base has a pontil mark and the neck and everted rim were tooled after the phial left the mould.

Window Glass

The next largest assemblage of glass after the bottle glass was the window glass. Apart from the medieval window glass cited above, fragments were of an early 18th to 19th century date. Eight bullions ("bull's eyes") were recovered. Bullions are the central boss where the pontil rod was attached to a pane of crown glass. Crown window glass is made by blowing a bubble of glass and transfering it to the pontil. The bubble is then cut open and rapidly rotated until, by centrifugal force, it was spread into a large disc up to 4 feet in diameter. This process was called the "Normandy method", believed to have been developed in Normandy in the 14th century, although this process was known to the Romans (Newman 1987, p.82). Crown window glass was being produced in England by migrant Norman glass-working families at least from the mid 16th century (Kenyon 1967, pp.82-87). When in 1615 the Royal "Proclamation touching glasses" forbade the use of wood for firing furnaces and making glass, one of the main areas of production for crown glass became Newcastle-upon-Tyne.

Figure 2:12 is an example of the bullions found at Coupée Lane and can be broadly dated to the 18th century. The absence of glazing marks on this and the unillustrated bullions suggests the possibility that crown glass was imported into Guernsey as complete "crowns" for later cutting. There is a reference that between July 1743 and July 1744 just over 4 tons of white glass were exported from Newcastle into Guernsey (Rush 1987, p.35). However, this is rather vague as white glass refers to vessel as well as window glass; therefore this hypothesis needs further research.

Fragments of glass quarries were also recovered. These consisted of nine quarry fragments, one complete quarry with lead shadow and one quarry set in lead cames (fig.1:13). The quarries are all triangular shaped and are probably of a late 17th - mid 18th century date, as casement windows (from which quarries came) pre-date sash windows which were first introduced into England in the late 17th century (Davies, p.78).

Conclusion

The Coupée Lane site proved to be important, both as a rare example of a local natural resource being dug for commercial reasons and for its artefactual evidence. Although the nature of the glass assemblage is very fragmentary and only four of the fragments of luxury glass pre-date the 18th century, it indicates that Guernsey was importing luxury, domestic and window glass at least from the medieval period onwards. The types recovered suggest that in this area of town, people were using contemporary forms of glass as they became available and as they were being used elsewhere.

The Illustrated Glass

Editor's Note

CL89 and CL92 refer to the seasons of excavation of Coupeé Lane which will be fully reported in the site publication (forth coming).

1.   Fragment from the body of a small flask or phial. The glass is much decayed and weathered to a dark brown. ? originally colourless glass with a green/yellow tint. Optic blown with 1mm raised ribbing. Possibly French. Medieval. CL92 T3 L3.

2.   Fragment from the bowl of a free blown goblet or beaker. Colourless cristallo glass with some seeding. Decorated with an applied and tooled vertical trail. 16th century. CL89 T2 L1 F2.

3.   ? Bugle bead. Blue glass with dark brown surface weathering. 18th century. CL89 T2 L1 EXT.

4.   Fragment from the base of a free blown stemmed wine glass. Colourless glass. Domed and folded foot rim. Mid 18th century. CL89 T2 F3.

5.   Base and part of a body of a square-sectioned case bottle. Pale olive green glass, much weathered. Mid 18th century. CL89 T2 F3.

6.   Neck, rim and part shoulder of a mallet bottle. Olive green glass, much weathered. Mid 18th century. CL89 T2 F9.

7.   Neck and rim of a free blown small wine bottle. Olive green glass with some weathering. Coil-like string rim. Possibly French. Mid 18th century. CL89 T2 F9.

8.   Neck, rim and part shoulder of a mould blown cylindrical wine bottle. Olive green glass, much weathered. Early 19th century. CL89 T2 L1.

9.   Complete free blown cylindrical phial with everted rim. Approximately 3 fl.oz. capacity. Colourless glass with natural green tint, some surface weathering. Slight hummock shaped kick with pontil mark. Late 18th - early 19th century. CL89 T2 F10.

10.   Complete free blown cylindrical phial with sharply everted rim. Approximately 1½ fl.oz. capacity. Colourless glass with light surface weathering. Shallow hummock shaped kick with pontil mark. Late 18th early 19th century. CL89 T2 F10.

11.   Complete mould blown steeple shaped phial with everted rim. Approximately 2 fl.oz. Colourless glass with natural blue/green tint with some surface weathering. The base has a pontil mark. Early 19th century. CL89 T2 F10.

12.   Crown window glass bullion. Colourless glass with pale blue/green tint. Some surface weathering. The glass is 2mm thick at cut edge of bullion. 18th century. CL89 T2 F10.

13.   Triangular window quarry set in lead cames. Probably broadglass. Colourless glass with natural green tint. Glass and lead much decayed. Late 17th - early 18th century. CL89 T2 F10.

Bibliography

Carey, E.F. (ed.) (1933-36) "The Growth of St. Peter Port in the Early 19th Century. From the M.S. of the late F.C. Lukis, Esq." *Transactions La Société Guernesiaise*, Vol. XII. pp 153-170

Charleston, R.J. (1975) "The Glass" in Platt, C. and Colman-Smith, R. "*Excavations in Medieval Southampton* 1953-1969, Vol.II, The Finds". Leicester University Press.

Charleston, R.J. (1984) "The Glass" in Allan, J.P. "*Medieval and Post-Medieval Finds from Exeter*, 1971-1980". Exeter Archaeol. Rep. 3.

Charleston, R.J. (1984) "*English Glass and the Glass used in England*, c.400 1940". Allen and Unwin.

Charleston, R.J. (1992) "The Glass" in Horsey, I.P. "*Excavations in Poole*, 1973-1983". Dorset Natural History and Archaeological Society Monograph Series. No.10.

Cox, C. (1907) "St. Peter Port in Bygone Times". *Transactions La Société Guernesiaise.* Vol.V. pp 333-348

Crellin, J.K. and Scott, J.R. *"Pharmaceutical History and its Sources in the Wellcome Collections.* III. Fluid Medicines, Prescription Reform and Posology, 1700-1900"

Davies, I. *"Window Glass in Eighteenth Century Williamsburg".*

Dumbrell, R. (1983) *"Understanding Antique Wine Bottles".* Antique Collectors Club.

Foy, D. (1989) *"Le verre médiéval et son artisanat en France Méditerranéenne".* Centre National de le Recherche Scientifique.

Kenyon, G.H. (1967) *"The Glass Industry of the Weald."* Leicester University Press.

Le Patourel, J.H. (1933-36) "The Early History of St. Peter Port." *Transactions La Société Guernesiaise.* Vol. XII.pp 171 - 208

Foy, D. and Sennequier, G. (1989) *À travers le verre du moyen âge à la renaissance."* Rouen.

Newman, H. (1987) *"An Illustrated Dictionary of Glass."* Thames and Hudson.

Rush, J. (1987) *"A Beilby Odyssey."* Nelson and Saunders.

Shepherd, J. (1994) " *The Vessel Glass."* in Watkins, D.R. "The Foundry. Excavations on Poole Waterfront. 1986-1987". Dorset Natural History and Archaeological Society. Monograph Series. No 14.

Wilkinson, O.N. (1968) *"Old Glass".* Benn.

Scale All 1:2

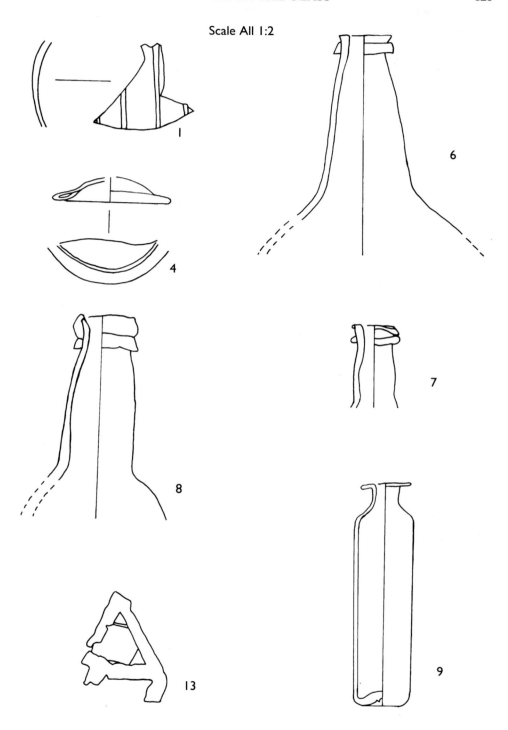

Figure 1.

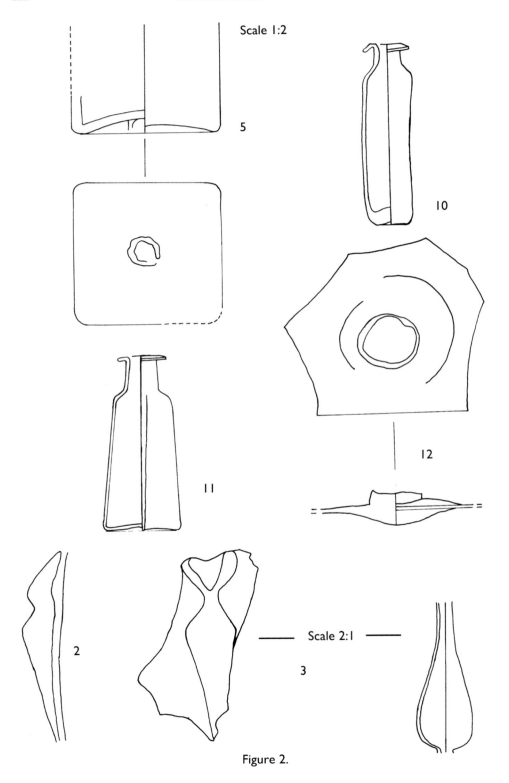

Scale 1:2

Scale 2:1

Figure 2.

A Late Sixteenth Century Shipwreck off Alderney

An interim report on the pre-disturbance survey

BY

MICHAEL BOWYER

Project Background

Alderney has a long history of ships being wrecked off its rugged coast, from prehistoric times to the present day, in what is probably the busiest shipping lane in northern European waters. In 1970, the site of an historic wreck was first brought to the attention of the Alderney diving club when an island fisherman, on recovering his fishing gear, found a large piece of concretion snagged in his lines. This concretion was almost dismissed and thrown back into the sea but at the last moment it was decided to it bring ashore and have it examined, by removing the hard covering of sand and marine growth. When this was done the salvaged item was identified as a musket. At the time, this was incorrectly thought to be dated to the nineteenth century and of little importance. The artefact remained on the island for several years; legend has it hanging on a pub wall. The story is that it was given, or more likely sold, to a foreign gentleman and appears to be lost to Alderney.

In 1990 members of the Alderney sub aqua club persuaded the fisherman to return to the area. They dived to a depth of some thirty metres to the sea bed. To their amazement they had landed on two cannon lying parallel about a metre apart. On further examination the divers discovered, in an area of sea bed 35 metres by 20 metres, more evidence to support the theory that this was indeed a ship wreck. This area off the Alderney coast was known as an anchorage far into the past. Evidence for this, when the only island harbour was at Longy Bay, is provided in a painting displayed in the entrance of the States Offices in St Anne. This is dated 11th June 1746 and was painted by Nicholas Dobrée of Guernsey. Thus it is quite possible that when excavation of the site begins, artefacts from ships from a much later period than the sixteenth century hull will also be discovered.

Over the following two years, the Alderney group carried out a provisional site survey to define the perimeters of the site and continued to lift any artefacts lying exposed on the sea bed. The team raised almost 1,000 artefacts, over half of which consisted of both pot sherds and almost complete pots. Two items were almost intact, one being an almost complete German salt-glazed stoneware jar or Bellarmine (see photograph) and the other a finely made pot thought to be a fire pot. A sherd of pottery material similar to the fire pot has been examined by an industrial chemist, to assess the black substance that stains the inside of the pot, the results of which initially suggest that the substance was not an inflammable material. Therefore it is possible that this pot was used for a different purpose. Further research is needed.

The pottery was handed to Bob Burns for examination. His immediate reaction was to reassess the date of the wreck site, from the nineteenth century to the sixteenth century. This astounding information meant that the site and how to proceed needed to be rethought. The wreck site now achieved a significance previously unthought, of due to the rarity of vessels of this period. By this time, the site had been intruded by another team of divers and so action to protect the site in law became a priority. The Receiver of Wrecks on Alderney was notified and the wreck was brought under the protection of The Wreck and Salvage (Vessels and Aircraft) (Bailiwick of Guernsey) Law 1986. This also required the States to become involved in the wreck administration. In 1993 the writer was appointed Project Director and Archaeologist with the brief to carry out a survey of the wreck site, begin a conservation programme on the raised artefacts, research the history of the wreck and raise a team of highly motivated, qualified, and unpaid archaeologists who specialised in the area of underwater archaeology. In this the writer was able to bring in students who were reading for a degree in Marine Archaeology at University of Wales at Bangor. The team also had the expert help of a number of people who had worked on wreck sites around the world. They were all amateur archaeologists but very experienced in the relatively new academic discipline of underwater archaeology.

The Wreck Site

The wreck site is some 400 metres off the north coast of Alderney in an area shown as "The Ledge" on marine charts. It is totally exposed to the prevailing winds and tidal currents which can reach 7 knots. With all these conditions combined with the depth, the dive time on a first dive of the working day is 19 minutes within a maximum of a 40 minutes window. If a second dive is undertaken within 24 hours, this is restricted to 12 minutes. To avoid the diving team being required to undertake long periods of decompression and, in the interests of safety, all divers undertake a 5 minute decompression stop at 10 metres. Underwater visibility can vary from 2 to 15 metres.

The wreck is lying east to west. The ship's rudder was recovered from the western end of the site. At mid tide, at the eastern end of the site the depth of water averages 28 metres whereas the western end of the site drops away in excess of 30 metres. The remains of the hull appear to be covered in sand varying in depth averaging from half to one and a half metres. This can alter with the tides. As seen in video evidence, a wave of sand approximately 40 cms in height moves across the site with each tide, on occasions covering artefacts then exposing them again on the next tide. Air probing has identified ship's timbers throughout the centre of the site although the depth of sand is unknown. It is assumed that a large amount of the ship's keel and the remains of frames including timbers, are still buried. The quantity can only be speculated on. Excavation will eventually provide the answers.

Artefacts

Artefacts raised between 1990 and 1993 have been stored in the old stables on the harbour. This building is very large and has provided a very suitable working area as it always has a cool temperature, thanks to the generosity of the Guernsey Maritime Trust who loaned the project a large collapsible holding tank. Artefacts that had been left out of water did not dry quickly:air drying is one of the less technical methods of conservation. In these cool conditions the survival rate was much higher than could have been expected in a warmer environment.

As noted the largest group of artefacts were ceramics. Identification and assessment started by Bob Burns was continued by Bob Thomson of Southampton after Bob Burns withdrew from further involvement in the project due to ill-health. The pottery dates to the second half of the sixteenth century. Other artefacts are personal possessions, ship's fittings and what appears to be a cargo of arms and armour.

Although all the artefacts can be tentatively dated to the second half of the sixteenth century, so far none have produced any evidence that could establish the identity of the ship or its intended destination. Only one artefact, a pewter porringer, has any markings that have produced a line of research. This is the name of its presumed owner: A .De. Bource. Initial research on the porringer likens it to others of Dutch origin. The name A. De. Bource has Dutch and French connections, possibly from Northern France. The name appears to have been spelt four different ways, although that is not unusual for the period. One other artefact lifted from the site before 1993 is a pewter wine flask. Early research places this to Northern France or The Low Countries.

The type and quality of several of the excavated artefacts suggest that this ship was not just a normal coastal trading vessel going about its daily business. The high status of several artefacts such as the pewter porringer and wine flask suggest that some of the cargo consisted of the personal possessions of persons of rank. Other items include ivory, possibly part of a fan, pewter spoons with the English rose motif and one pewter screw cap from a glass bottle. This type of bottle was usually quite decorative. Examples of these have recently been recovered from a wreck off the Dutch coast, report as yet unpublished.

Two other artefacts are of considerable interest. One is a pewter smoking pipe believed to be the only one known dating from the 16th century. The second is a pair of stirrups. When recovered these were still gilded indicating that they had been buried in the seabed until excavated. This would also suggest that the ship was carrying horse harness. They have been examined by pewter specialists who have suggested that if further conservation is undertaken, some of the original decoration can be recovered. Other personal artefacts include a hair comb and leather shoes. There were also 36 animal bones, several of which have butchery marks. These bones are from cattle, pigs, goats and sheep and were probably packed in barrels.

The two artefacts that have placed the wreck into a much smaller time frame within the second half of the 16th century have been the two merchant or pan weights. The first if these is 454.0g (1.009 lb) in weight and the second is 906.5 g (1.9985 lb). Both are marked with the crowned EL alongside a sword. Research by Brian Smith, a member of the archaeological team, dates these to the reign of Elizabeth I, and the stamps provide the dating for the wreck to between 1587 and 1602.

During the four working seasons between 1993 and 1996 that the archaeological team, brought in by the States of Alderney, worked on the site survey, two major artefacts and six small items were brought to the surface. Several were in danger of being destroyed by the action of weather and tides. If these items had been destroyed any information that may have come from these would certainly have been lost. The first major artefact excavated was a cannon. The decision to lift it was based, not only on its significance, but also that it was still attached to its carriage. If the ship should turn out to be English and from the latter half of the sixteenth century then the gun carriage would be a very exclusive and unique artefact. A very excited member of the Royal Armouries, explained that no gun carriages from an English ship of this period had survived to the present day. Thus how guns were mounted on ships, the design and construction of carriages was, and still is, a mystery.

The excavated cannon is 7feet 8 inches in length with a bore of 4 ins. The weight of the cannon is stamped on the barrel and is 1400 lbs. (Note, the weight and dimensions are in imperial, as they were originally). This artefact was loaded and ready to fire. When the tampion was removed the inside of the barrel was still dry- some 400 years after it had been prepared for action. The cannon and carriage will be returned to Alderney for display in 1998.

Dating and timbers

In 1996 a proposal was taken to the States Members to excavate the one artefact that could provide the vital information for the dimensions of the ship's hull. The reasons for the excavation of this very important item, namely the ship's rudder, were two fold, firstly, the ability of the rudder to suggest the size of the hull and secondly during the three years that the rudder had been monitored the timber was decaying in parts to the point that it could have been totally destroyed. Permission was granted and the rudder lifted. It was later removed to York where it is undergoing examination and a full programme of conservation. A full report is yet to be published although the rudder has been the subject of a television documentary where the process of diagnosing the dimensions of the hull was demonstrated. At that time dendrochronology, the dating of wood from the growth rings, was attempted. Unfortunately there were not enough rings to give an accurate result.

In the early years of the project the Alderney diving team had lifted what are thought to be two hatch covers. One of these was taken to Sheffield University, where specialists in dendrochronology did find enough growth rings to produce suggested dates. The timber was still growing in 1550 and by estimating the rings of the sap wood it is suggested that the tree from which the timber was taken was felled sometime around 1583/6. Again this narrows the historic time frame. If these are from this wreck and fitted when the ship was built, then the date of wrecking in 1592 is a possibility. It must be noted as a matter of caution however that there is no firm evidence to confirm that these hatches actually came from this ship wreck. As noted above, the area was an old anchorage and these timbers could have been jettisoned from another ship.

Historic Research

With a date placing the wreck to a time window in the latter half of the sixteenth century, (from the dating of the ceramics), historic research began into the maritime history of Alderney, Guernsey and Jersey. Research in the PRO (Public Records Office) records that a ship was cast away about Alderney in 1592 carrying dispatches from Queen Elizabeth's first minister, Lord Burghley to Sir John Norreys who was opposing, an army of 4,000 Spanish troops. Norreys' army had landed in Brittany in 1591 to support the Catholic League.

Whilst the history of England's sea battle and the defeat of the Spanish Armada in 1588 is known to every schoolchild, what is less well known is Philip of Spain's continued obsession, to again return England to the Catholic faith. This period in Northern Europe was dominated by dramatic change caused by religious and civil conflict between the Protestants of the North and the Catholics in the South. During this period, and at the time of the wreck off Alderney recorded in the PRO, the Low Countries were under the influence of Spain. The French King, was at first a Protestant, although he converted to Catholicism in 1593 and continued to oppose the Spanish until they were eventually defeated by a joint English and French army commanded by Sir John Norreys at Crozon, near Brest, in 1594.

Throughout the period of England's involvement in the campaign its army was continually being reinforced and supplied from England and the Low Countries. Many of these ships would call at Guernsey and Jersey the two largest of the group that make up the Channel Islands. Ships making passage from the South of England ports and Northern Europe would pass close to Alderney with its treacherous coast line and surrounding seas.

The Project

From its inception it has always been the intention of those involved in the project to identify the remains of the ship and glean any information that could throw any light on ships and sea faring from this period. This research will continue but it is very time consuming as this may require visits to archives not only in England but most certainly in France and Holland.

With this project Alderney now has the opportunity to place on record its maritime history. There is no reason to doubt that it was an active island involved in maritime trade, as were all the Channel Islands. Certainly the Romans settled on the island and it is very possible that the remains of their ships still remain to be found. With the establishment of marine archaeology studies on Alderney these possibilities could become a reality.

This project has many problems not least because of the depth at which the wreck is lying. To run a field programme over a two week period on Alderney is logistically very difficult. A field team consists of up to sixteen staff. Getting all the equipment to keep the field team operating at full strength on to the island means flying in staff and small items of equipment. To have the large pieces of equipment such as boats, diving equipment, survey equipment and diving compressors on the island at the right time requires having this shipped on the weekly supply boat from Weymouth. This task alone is demanding. Due to the remoteness of the island, it is necessary to have all equipment backed up with spares to cope with any breakdown. A lost day can never be made up. Because of the depth and the necessity to go into decompression after each dive, a diver can do no more than six dives in three days. The build up of nitrogen in the body can reach dangerous levels possibly resulting in decompression sickness. Unfortunately the island does not have a decompression chamber. Any diver suspected of having an embolism has to be flown off the island to Guernsey. Flying at any height and the time taken to deliver the diving casualty to a chamber is critical. Safety, therefore is the highest priority of the project.

Conclusion

Whilst the original thoughts on what the shipwreck may have been have now been discounted, we do have a little more information on the dimensions of the hull from the recovery of the ship's rudder and part of the stern post. What we are now looking for is a hull that is some 30ft longer than the Makeshift, the ship first named by David Keys in 1992 and on which a great amount of research has now been done. Although it is now known not to be that pinnace, the research has produced valuable information on the part played by these fast hulls during the Brittany campaign. Pinnaces were ideally suited to blockading ports and estuaries and as fast supply packets. These ships were designed and used to make fast passages, carrying dispatches and people who needed to be somewhere in a hurry. A Pinnace could have been carrying the two packets from

Burghley to Norreys in the ship cast away in February 1592 off Alderney. It is still not proven that the Alderney wreck was the one noted in the States Papers in the PRO. Hopefully future work on the wreck will eventually yield enough information to reveal its identity.

Acknowledgements

I should like to express my grateful thanks to the many people without whose hard work and co-operation the project could not have achieved so much. Projects such as the Alderney wreck project can only succeed when the members of the team work together for the good of the project. This effort was without reward, other than seeing their efforts on display for all to enjoy. Bodies who always supported the project during the tenure of the writer include, The States of Alderney who backed the project with financial aid and the several commercial companies from the mainland and those who are resident on Alderney, namely, Aurigny, Channel Seaways and Alderney Electric. Others who gave their time and considerable effort include the members of The Alderney Sub Aqua Club and the Friends of the Wreck chaired by Sherry Milan. My grateful thanks to them also. I should like to thank my team of specialists who came over from the mainland to impart their skills to make the project a success. Lastly my thanks to the people who I turned to for advice when I needed a second opinion, Heather Sebire, Guernsey Museum and Bob Thomson of Southampton. My lasting thanks go to two people who gave me and the project their total support and appointed me to the post of Director and Archaeologist, David Jenkins, from Alderney and my mentor Bob Burns, formerly of Guernsey Museum. To all my heartfelt thanks.

Bibliography

Hakluyt R 1926 *The Principle Voyages Traffiques and Discoveries of the English Nation 1552-1616.*

MacCaffrey W.T. 1992 *Elizabeth I: War and Politics 1588-1603* Princeton.

Smith B.S. 1997 Inquiry into two lead weights found on a wreck in Alderney, Channel Islands *The International Journal of Nautical Archaeology* 26.2 p133-143.

Wernham R. B. (ed). 1984 *List and analysis of States Papers Foreign Series Elizabeth 1* vol.iv, H.M.S.O.

W. Boek 1993 *Dictionary of Belgium and Northern France, Family Names* . Brussels

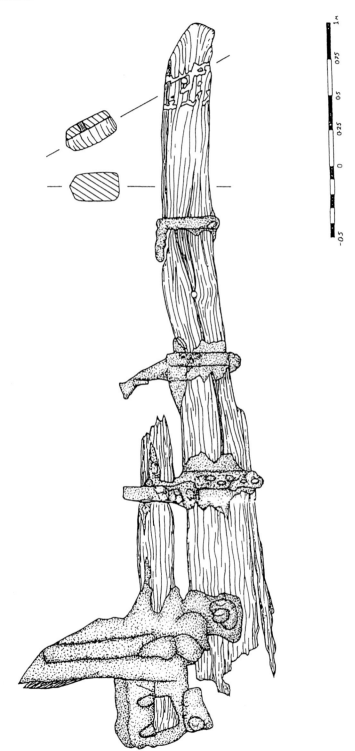

The rudder of the late 16th Century Shipwreck off Alderney
Illustration: Doug McElvougue.

Guernsey Folk in old Southampton

BY

DUNCAN H. BROWN

It has seldom been easy to bridge the gap between archaeological evidence and real people. History is full of names, archaeology is full of things, and bringing the two together is not only difficult, it is all too often discouraged. The act of excavation gives a thrill of discovery and inspires the imagination. Yet these moments are far removed from the dry discourses published as archaeological analysis. Convention has created a gap between feeling and writing. Fortunately, Bob Burns is not a conventional man. He would, I hope, feel complimented by my suggestion that he feels more than he writes. He has always been a raconteur, a story-teller. The past, for Burns, is something to be understood with the heart as much as the head, and who would find fault with that?

This paper should, therefore, tell a story and so bridge the gap between history and archaeology, between convention and fancy. The fact that it falls short of this is perhaps a comment on the nature of the evidence. My sources are principally documentary, so I am already flouting convention by studying history as an archaeologist, as well as by writing in the first person. In this paper I have tried to bring together references to Guernsey folk in the published records of 15th century Southampton. I have drawn from four sources: the Port Books, the Stewards' Books, the Black Book, and the Terrier of 1454. These are all 15th century documents and represent a tiny fraction of the wealth of historical sources available to the student of late medieval Southampton. There are not many references to Guernsey folk but there are several specific to the same individual, around whom a story may be told.

Guernsey folk at sea

The port books are customs accounts, a record of the shipping that passed through the port of Southampton and the dues that were payable on the cargoes. The account was kept by the water-bailiff for a year which usually ran from Michaelmas to Michaelmas. These documents provide a colourful insight into the business of the port and they show a wonderful variety of the goods handled there. Guernsey traders are not, unfortunately, identified very often in the port books. At least this means they can all be listed here.

The earliest published references to Guernsey boats are to be found in the port book for the year 1427-28 (Studer 1913). The third entry for that year is *la Michele of Guernsey*, with John de Maresk its master (ibid, 4). The cargo included conger eels, *oulone* (a type of cloth), crestcloth and linen. The vessel left the same day loaded with flax. A few days later *la Katherine* entered port, with Peter Le

Blank as master and carrying conger eels and linen (*ibid*, 8). She was closely followed by *le Passemoket*, mastered by Michael Le Orlu, which had previously docked at Lymington (ibid, 10). Canvas, crestcloth, oulone, linen and quilts comprised the goods unloaded. *Le Gracieu*, master John Gaynepain, was brought in towards the end of February 1428 with a cargo of wine and canvas (*ibid*, 33). A consignment of crestcloth was recorded as having been unloaded at Langstone. The master John de Maresk returned in the spring of 1428 aboard a different boat, *la Marie*, with conger eels and linen (*ibid*, 40). In the same season *la Gylyenne* arrived, mastered by Piere Gosse, anchored at Calshot and left with a cargo of alum (*ibid*, 72). A few days later *le Larron*, with master John Petyot, brought mackerel, onions, wine and canvas (*ibid*, 73). *La Marguyte* arrived in the summer of 1428 with Guylliam Papain as master with wine consigned to a certain Thomas Florys (*ibid*, 55). On the return journey, made the same day, wine, fruit, herring, resin, pitch and alum, coal and two 'sacks of bowls', presumably of wood, were carried on behalf of the same Thomas Florys. A further load of fruit, herring, pitch and alum was consigned to Robert Florys, who was the water-bailiff compiling the customs accounts for that year.

Robert Florys appears again in the spring of 1428 as consignee for wine and iron brought on a Southampton boat, *le Crisofre*. He is also named as one who gave pledge for the, supposedly temporary, non-payment of dues. This practice was prohibited but, as pledgers' names were often recorded in the port books, apparently overlooked. In the late summer of 1428 he paid for items consigned to, among others, Walter Fetplace, the Mayor of Southampton.

There are just three references for the accounting year 1435-36. The earliest is for November 1435, when the *Jesus of Guernsey*, mastered by Guillame Henr', brought in 600 conger eels, 200 ells of canvas and 100 ells of linen cloth (Foster 1963, 6). A month later, in December, Denys du Rochier, master of the *Trovendu* of Guernsey, unloaded wine, crestcloth, linen and wheat. He left port the same day, with wine, fruit and lead (*ibid*, 14). In August 1436 *le Nicol de Guernsey*, under master Pierres Thomas, brought in canvas, crestcloth, conger eels, garlic and wick yarn, all consigned to Thomas Florys. A further load of canvas, crestcloth and linen was consigned to Pieres Clement.

The port book for 1439-40 is slightly more productive. On the 29th October 1439, master 'Willelmi Harries de Gernesye' unloaded canvas and wool-cards (Cobb 1961, 10). Stephanus Bygod docked on the 1st December with crestcloth, broadcloth, canvas, quilts, wine and conger eels (*ibid*. 15). On the 18th of April 1440 Thomas Quyntyn, master of a 'batella de Gerneseye' carried in a consignment of wine, salt, quilts, fur mantles and wick-yarn for Thomas Florys (*ibid*. 43). Quyntyn visited again ten days later with more merchandise for Thomas Florys, this time coal, linen and kersyes, or narrow cloth (*ibid*. 45). The 14th June 1440 saw Quyntyn return, on behalf of the same merchant, with 30 quarters of wheat (*ibid*. 48). William Florye, another consignee, might have been related and thus may also be a Guernseymen. On the 18th March 1439, feather-beds, napery and shears were unloaded on his behalf (*ibid*. 409). More feather-beds were imported in his name on the 1st August 1440 (*ibid*. 52) and on the 1st September, ginger.

Robert Florys is recorded as giving pledge on two occasions in these accounts. On the 14th January 1439, a ship of Barfleur brought barley, beans, wheat and rope for Johanne Rewatt. Robert Florys stood pledge for total dues of six shillings and a penny (*ibid*. 24). Almost a year later, on the 4th January 1440, Thomas Barbour of Lowestoft brought a ship-load of herring for which Robert Florys pledged custom and wharfage (*ibid*. 109). The amounts due are not recorded and it may be that these sums were never paid.

These are the only 15th-century port book entries that refer specifically to vessels and merchants of Guernsey. This is perhaps surprising, given the strength of the links between the island and Southampton that survive today. One explanation for the apparent lack of Guernsey names may be that many of the more frequent visitors to Southampton were often mentioned by name only, and their origins go unrecorded. Thomas Quyntyn docked three times in 1440, but is only once identified as being of Guernsey (*ibid*. 43). Another reason might be the preference of Guernsey for the port of Poole over Southampton. This is stated in 1515 in an agreement made with the merchants of Guernsey whereby the custom and wharfage they paid was reduced. This is explained as an attempt to attract their business away from Poole (Third Book of Remembrance I, 27-8). This preference for the Dorset port may be reflected in ceramic assemblages excavated there. Jarvis has commented that 'in the late 14th/15th century Poole has a relatively large assemblage of Normandy wares when compared with Southampton and elsewhere' Jarvis (1992, 62).

Quantified data from Poole comparable with that compiled for Southampton is not available for the same numbers of excavations. However, this author has observed that certain Normandy pottery types, especially Developed Normandy Gritty ware and related products occur with greater frequency in Poole than they do in Southampton. Furthermore, Spoerry has shown that French pottery represents nearly 50% by weight of all the late medieval imported Continental wares from the Foundry excavations on Poole waterfront (Spoerry1994, 48, fig.38). The comparative figure from the combined assemblages of nine Southampton sites is 19% (Brown, 1993, 78). No mention is made in the port books of pottery arriving on Guernsey boats, but their most common cargo, cloth, was made in Normandy as well as on the islands. Guernsey merchants relied especially on canvas as a staple and imported pottery tends to follow principal trade routes. Developed Normandy Gritty ware was first identified in the assemblage from Château de Marais (Thomson 1980) and the author has observed this ware in significant quantities at Castle Cornet and elsewhere. Poole of course thrived on direct trade with Normandy as well as Guernsey, but frequent finds of the same ceramic products in both places suggests that some of the pottery found in the Dorset port was brought by Channel Islanders.

The character of the Guernsey merchants and boat-masters is not revealed in the documents, but the nature of their work is. They dealt mainly in cloth of all kinds, supplemented with wine and fish. It is probable that Guernsey boats, once they had crossed from their home island, plied their trade down and along the south coast, calling in at various ports. Two references in the Stewards Books of Southampton may confirm this image. These contain the public accounts, as maintained by the town Steward, and list items of expenditure. The accounts of William Fletcher for the year 1433-4, contain two references to one John Guernsey. On one occasion 'he and his mates' were paid seven pence for hiring a boat and for towing timber from Itchen to Westhythe' (Gidden 1935, 77). John Guernsey and his mates later received another seven pence for 'a leather strap for his boat loaded with timber' (*ibid.* 137). John may not have been of Guernsey, but it is tempting to think of him as being so. The remainder of this paper is concerned with another, less uncertain Guernsey connection.

Guernsey folk in town

Among the scattered references to Guernseymen in the port books, the name Florys occurs regularly. William Florye was a consignee who appears only twice, in the accounts for 1439-40, and his links with the Florys name are unsubstantiated. We are on a surer footing with Thomas Florys, another merchant whom we know was related to Robert, resident of Southampton and giver of pledges. It is the story of Robert Florys that is to be told here. The relationship between Robert and Thomas is established in Robert's will. This was made in December 1443 and bequeathed to '*Thomas Florice (sic), my kinsman, the son of Thomas Florice of Guernsey, my two tenements, with all their appurtenances*' (Chapman 1912, 137). This document is contained in the Black Book of Southampton, where Robert Florys makes further appearances. On May 8th 1425 he signed as witness to a release and he was present at further court proceedings in 1427, 1435 and 1442. The 1435 case was held to establish proof of age for one Katerina Jamys, widow of Drewet Payn at seventeen years. Robert Florys, with eleven others, declared '*upon their oath that the aforesaid Katerina is fifteen years of age and more ... and each of the said twelve burgesses says separately that he himself was then living in the aforesaid town* [of Southampton]' (*ibid.* 59).

Robert can therefore be identified as a burgess, an influential and presumably wealthy townsman. His court appearance of 1427 gives more detail. The King's common court was held before '*Walter Fetplace, mayor, John Estewelle and Robert Florys, bailiffs on the Tuesday after St Hillary's day, 5 Henry VI* [Tuesday 16th January 1427]' (*ibid.* 41). This leads us back to the port books, which show that he was bailiff in 1426-27 and again in 1435-6. It was he, therefore, who recorded the cargo of canvas, crestcloth, eels, garlic and yarn delivered in 1436 aboard the *Nicol de Guernsey* and consigned to his own kinsman, Thomas Florys. A small mistake, made in the same port book, adds humanity to his official appearances in the documents. The *Jesus of Guernsey* mentioned above was mastered by Guillame Henr', but the name of Thomas Florys was written in first and crossed out (Foster 1963, 6). This poignant detail suggests that the arrival of a boat from Guernsey reminded him of his relative, and perhaps his home.

The nature of that relationship, and Robert's origins, are not clear. There are two Thomases, the inheritor of Robert's estate and his father, 'Thomas Florice of Guernsey'. It is possible that Robert and his heir, or he and the elder Thomas, were brothers; the relationship seems close. What is known is that there was a Guernsey merchant named Thomas Florys. It is thus tempting to think of Robert as a Guernseymen also, who made good perhaps, after arriving in Southampton to further the family concerns. The sending abroad of relatives was a common enough practice among merchant families, and still is. His own status as a merchant is confirmed in the port book of 1428, by his office as bailiff and his role as a pledger for other traders. It seems less likely that Thomas represents the process in reverse, as there were more lucrative places than Guernsey to seek one's fortune in the 15th century. The fact that *'Thomas Florice, my kinsman, the son of Thomas Florice of Guernsey'* was bequeathed Robert's Southampton tenements indicates that he had no surviving relatives on the mainland. This might be further evidence that he was also of Guernsey. His will states that his wife, Elena, had died before him. There is no mention. of any children. It is possible that Elena died in 1436, for it was then that a chantry was founded in her name, and that of her husband (Davies, 1883 424). A chantry was an annual stipend to the priest to fund the saying of a mass in somebody's name. Robert Florice stipulated the saying of such a mass in his will, but the chantry was obviously created before his final wishes were recorded. The chantry was founded in the church of St. Michael's, the principal church of the town, for February the 22nd.

Robert's will certainly confirms him as a man of substance. He owned two tenements. One was in 'le Bulstrete', now Bugle Street, the central thoroughfare of the prosperous south-west quarter of Southampton. It was here that the town's wealthiest burgesses and merchants lived, as is testified by the substantial vaulted stone cellars that survive to-day in great numbers. His other property was a tenement in a street identified in his will as 'the Fysshe Markett', and now known as Blue Anchor Lane. This runs down from Bugle Street to the area where the medieval quays were. The Southampton Terrier of 1454, a list of all the properties and their owners in the town, mentions both tenements (Burgess, 1976). The one in 'le Bulstrete' is described in Robert's will as *'between the tenement of the Prior....of St. Denys....on the north side, and the tenement of Marjory Mascall on the south side; and it extends from the aforesaid street on the east to Ronceval* [another property] *on the west'*. The Terrier description for plot 365 is *'The tenement of the Mayor and Commonalty of the town of Southampton, late of Robert Florys....* ' (*ibid* 101). To the north are holdings of the Prior of St. Denys, Terrier numbers 366-369, while number 364 to the south is described as *'the small tenement.... late of Marjory Mascall'*. The 'Fysshe Markett' property is also easy to locate. Robert's will places it between *'the tenement of the Abbot and Convent of Beaulieu.... and the tenement of John Tyer....'.* The Terrier does not mention John Tyer, but plot number 384 is entered as the 'cottage of John William, late of Robert Florys, that John Hambury now holds' (*ibid* 105). The adjacent land, Terrier number 385, is described as *'The tenement of the Abbot and Convent of*

Beaulieu'. The Terrier also mentions Robert Florys once more, as holder of a tenement just south of his property in 'le Bulstrete'. Terrier number 363 is described as *'The vacant plot of the Prior and Convent of St. Denys.... that Robert Florys lately acquired from them for a term of years....'* (*ibid*, 101). This rented plot naturally was not bequeathed in Robert's will but it is clear that he has considerable concerns in Southampton.

Sadly, there is no mention in the Terrier of Thomas Florys, the heir to these possessions. Robert's will states that *'.... if it happen that the aforesaid Thomas dies without an heir male....or if it happen that the same said Thomas.... shall in any way hinde the execution of my last will, and shall not fulfil my same will as abovesaid then I will give and grant that the mayor and corporation of the aforesaid town shall enter on, possess and hold the two aforesaid tenements.... '*. It seems that Thomas either died without a son, or failed to uphold the conditions of the will, for the Terrier identifies the town as the owners of tenement number 365. These were simply that he should cause a mass to be said annually in remembrance of Robert and his wife. It is unlikely that Thomas would not do this, and he may therefore have been the last representative of the Florys family in Southampton. The chantry that Robert stipulated was still being paid for by the town in the reign of Edward VI, which suggests that his old properties had remained under corporate ownership (Davies, 426).

One of Robert's properties, the tenement in 'Fysshe Markett', was excavated in 1972 following the demolition of St. Michael's house (site code SOU 122). Unfortunately, the results have not been fully published, and only a few interim statements are available in print. A substantial length of street frontage, on the north side of Blue Anchor Lane was uncovered, running from Bugle Street, to the east and the town wall at the western end. The Terrier shows that several tenements were situated here, and the excavations have confirmed this. A number of stone-built footings for external walls and interior partitions were exposed and some of them doubtless relate to Robert's holding. The house on that particular tenement was shown to be small and probably insubstantial. Sadly, few finds can be attributed to this plot, as excavations concentrated on larger and more productive buildings close to the lower wall. Few significant features were found, and most of the finds in this area came from layers. However, a well-constructed stone-lined well was revealed in this part of the trench. It had been filled in sometime in the 18th century, but may have been dated from the medieval period. It is likely that Robert Florys did not occupy this site himself, and the Terrier entry also suggests this, as a number of different people are mentioned. The Terrier also refers to this plot as a cottage, rather than a tenement, which infers a lower status. The larger, acknowledged, tenement in 'le Bulstrete' is a more likely setting for the Florys home.

We are left with an enticingly incomplete picture of Robert Florys. He was a merchant, burgess and bailiff who lived in the most prosperous quarter of the town. He died a childless widower, leaving his possessions to the son of a close relative who was also a merchant and a Guernseymen. It is not certain that Robert Florys was from Guernsey himself, but the evidence does support this claim. Whatever the circumstances of his arrival in Southampton, he undoubtedly became an influential member of his adopted community.

Conclusion

Amidst historical fragments a story can be found. The nature of relations between Southampton and Guernsey, and the competing port of Poole, is attested in the documentary and archaeological evidence. One Guernseyman, the merchant Thomas Florys, must have been enticed to Southampton by the position of his kinsman, Robert, as bailiff. It is perhaps with some degree of faith, rather than certainty, that Robert Florys is identified as a Guernseymen, but of his place in Southampton's own history there can be no doubt. Another Robert made the same transition in reverse.

Bob Burns, Londoner, merchant seaman, property-owner, has made his own, immense, contribution to Guernsey's past. The French wine that we have consumed amidst the conviviality around his kitchen table has carried us through many historical deliberations, and fuelled many stories. The parallels with that earlier Robert are, like Bob's company, too attractive and I shall not dwell on them. I only hope that Burns enjoys the little tale that, this time, I have spun for him.

Bibliography

Barton, K J, 1980, Excavations at the Château des Marais (Ivy Castle), Guernsey, *Transactions of La Société Guernesiaise*, Vol XX, pp657-702

Brown, D H, 1993, *The Imported Pottery of Late Medieval Southampton*, Medieval Ceramics 17, pp77-81

Burgess, L A, 1976, *The Southampton Terrier of 1454*, Southampton Records Series XV

Cobb, H S, 1961, *The Local Port Book of Southampton 1439-40*, Southampton Records Series

Davies, J S, 1883, *A History of Southampton*, Southampton

Foster, B, 1963 *The Local Port Book of Southampton for 1435-36*, Southampton University Press

Gidden, H W, 1935, *The Stewards' Books of Southampton from 1428*, Vol I 1428-1434, Southampton Record Society

Chapman, A B W, 1912, *The Black Book of Southampton* Vol II, c. AD. 1414-1503, Southampton Record Society

Horsey, I P, 1939, *Excavations in Poole 1973-1983,* Dorset Natural History and Archaeological Society Monograph Series 10

Jarvis, K S, 1992, *Introduction to the Pottery* in Horsey, I P, 1992, pp62-65

Spoerry, P, 1994, *The Medieval and Post-Medieval Pottery.* in Watkins, D R, 1994, pp 45-51

Studer, P, 1913, *The Port Books of Southampton 1427-1430,* Southampton Record Society

Thomson, R G, 1980, *The Pottery* in Barton 1980, pp677—86

Watkins, D R, 1994, *The Foundry: Excavations on Poole Water-front 1986-87,* Dorset Natural History and Archaeological Society Monograph Series 14

Pebbles, Pots and Bangs: Three 18th Century Guernsey-Southampton Links

BY
ROBERT THOMSON

These three short notes are offered to Bob Burns as a small token in return for the many years of friendship that we have enjoyed. These are just three of the diverse subjects which Bob and I have spent hours discussing at his kitchen table at Elmleigh, usually helped by copious quantities of Côtes du Rhone.

Pebbles

Large (9"x 6"x 4"), smooth granite pebbles are a common find in the upper levels of archaeological sites in Southampton and Portsmouth and are frequently found built into 19th century and later garden walls in both towns. They have been dismissed in the past as being 'ships ballast' but they also occur in similar circumstances in Winchester, (Liz Lewis pers.comm), which is some distance from the sea and the pebbles must have been transported there deliberately. Bob Burns first suggested a possible Channel Island origin for the pebbles but was unable to suggest a reason for their presence in such large quantities on the mainland.

A paper on early 18th century street paving in London, (Jeffreys 1988) gave the clue to a hitherto unsuspected major trade link between Guernsey and the mainland. London streets in 1767 were to be paved 'with new pebble paving, not less than 14" deep...at 3s 6d per yard. The pebbles in each such yard ought to be 3 hundred weight', (Ibid p30). A later reference confirms their Channel Island origin: '...pebble paving, which is done with stones collected from the sea-beach, mostly brought from the islands of Guernsey and Jersey; they are very durable, indeed the most so of any stone used for this purpose. They are of various sizes, but those which are six to nine inches deep are esteemed the most serviceable.' (ibid).

Many thousands of tons of such pebbles would be necessary to pave London streets and must have been transported there as beneficial cargo. Pebbles make a very bulky and awkward load and can only have been shipped directly from Guernsey to London. The London paving contracts were let out to small contractors who were employed to pave a street to a given specification using their own materials. No documentation for these individual small contractors survives and the various contracts unfortunately only give costs for the total job and not the cost or source of the materials.

In Portsmouth, the Portsmouth Paving Commissioners issued specifications similar to the London ones to local paviors, again giving only overall costings. Several of the Portsmouth contracts survive (Portsmouth Record Office, PUS1/1), but the earliest of these, dated 5 October 1764, does not specify the materials to be used and a later one of 23 February 1768 specifies '...good Isle of Wight pebbles at '...one ton of such pebbles to four square yards' to be used. However a contract signed on 19 April 1768 specifies that 'The horseways and carriageways of the said streets [shall be paved with] good new Guernsey pebbles with not less than one ton of such pebbles to four square yards...' All subsequent Portsmouth contracts, at least until the 1820s, continue to specify Guernsey pebbles. Interestingly, the Portsmouth requirement of 5cwt to the square yard is somewhat more than the London specification of 3cwt to the square yard.

Winchester appointed its first Pavement Commissioners in 1771 and issued specifications based on those of Portsmouth and Gosport, including the use of Guernsey pebbles (Lewis 1993 p6). Southampton's first 18th century Paving Act was passed in 1770 and not only did Southampton copy Portsmouth specifications, they also appointed the Portsmouth surveyor, Richard Proate, and the Portsmouth pavoir, John Monday (Stovold 1990 p22). Many of Southampton's streets were already paved as the town's first paving act was passed in 1477 and a town pavior was appointed in 1482, (Davis 1883 p119). Much of this pre-18th century paving must have survived, albeit in a very poor state, as the contractor appointed under the 1770 Act was only required to re-use old materials; '...old Pebbles to be taken up and relaid' and 'the Commissioners will find any new pebbles that may be wanting', (Stovold 1990 p19).

There are several more references in the 1770 accounts to the Commissioners providing new materials at their own expense but it is not until 4 March 1772 that the first direct Guernsey stone-trader is identified. 'Ordered that Captain Priaulx do bring from Guernsey fifty Tons of Horse Flatners at the market price and that he is allowed 1s 6d per Ton freight. The Dimensions from 6 to 9 Inches in Depth & the same in Width', (Ibid p50). On 25 March Priaulx is ordered to bring 15 ton more of Guernsey horse flatners upon the same terms as before and on 8 April 1772 the Commission Treasurer, Mr Guilliame, is instructed to pay Joshua Judas £11 1s for 17 ton of Guernsey horse flatners at 11s 6d a ton for the stones and 1s 6d per ton freight, (Ibid p51). On 3 June 1772 he is ordered to pay Nicholas Priaulx £6 3s 4 $^1\backslash$2d for freight and charges on 63 tons of stone from Guernsey, (ibid p 52).

Various transactions dealing with Guernsey stone were summarised by the Treasurer for the Commission meeting of 1 December 1773 which, for the first time, gives some detail of the trade and the various individuals engaged in it.

Date	Names	Quantities	Sums paid

1771

Date	Names	Quantities	Sums paid
May 30	Capt Gallienne	42 tons	7 7 0
June 12	Capt Priaulx	31 $\frac{1}{2}$ tons	5 10 3
June 13	Capt Morant	24 tons 2 q	4 4 4
July 3	"	16 tons	2 16 0
July 10	W. Robinson	4 tons	16 0
July 26	Capt Gallienne	102 $\frac{1}{2}$ tons	17 18 9
Aug 1	Capt Fallaise	35 $\frac{1}{2}$ tons	6 4 3
Aug 21	Capt Morant	15 $\frac{1}{4}$ tons	2 13 4 $\frac{1}{2}$
Aug 24	Capt Priaulx	54 tons	9 9 0
Sept 7	Capt Gallienne	94 $\frac{1}{2}$ tons	16 9 10 $\frac{1}{2}$
Nov 1	Capt Judas	31 tons	5 8 6
Nov 15	Capt Morant	17 tons	2 19 6
Dec 21	Mr Tupper	6 tons	1 1 0

1772

Date	Names	Quantities	Sums paid
Mar 5	Capt Priaulx	42 tons	7 7 0
May 1	Judas	17 tons of Guernsey horse flatners and freight	11 1 0
May 16	Capt Lihou	23 $\frac{1}{2}$ tons pebbles	4 1 4
May 26	Capt Fallaise	49 $\frac{3}{4}$ tons pebbles	8 14 0
June 4	Priaulx for freight of 63 $\frac{3}{4}$ ton of Guernsey flatners		6 3 4 $\frac{1}{2}$
———	Priaulx for	3 $\frac{1}{2}$ tons pebbles	12 3
July 30	Paid Priaulx for	63 $\frac{3}{4}$ tons Guernsey flatners	35 1 0
Oct 14	Capt Gallienne	45 $\frac{3}{4}$ tons pebbles	8 0 0
Dec 9	Capt Priaulx	66 $\frac{1}{2}$ tons	11 12 9

1773

Date	Names	Quantities	Sums paid
? 18	Capt Gallienne	14 $\frac{3}{4}$ tons	2 11 7 $\frac{1}{2}$
Nov 15	Capt Priaulx	8 tons	1 8 0

This accounts for 3,876 $\frac{1}{4}$ tons of stone costing £179 1s 2d.
A further summary of 29 November 1775 accounted for a further 1 83 $\frac{3}{4}$ tons of stone (Ibid p78):

1773

Date	Names	Quantities	Sums paid
Dec 7	Capt Judas	11 tons	1 18 6

1774

Date	Names	Quantities	Sums paid
Feb 4	Mr Tho. Hammond	34 $\frac{3}{4}$ tons	6 1 7 $\frac{1}{2}$
Dec 5	Capt Morant	26 tons	4 11 0
Dec 5	Capt Priaulx	4 tons	14 0

Dec 5	Capt Judas	13 tons	2 5 6

1775

Oct 19	Capt Judas	34 tons	5 19 0
Nov 27	Mr Monday	26 tons	4 11 0
Nov 27	Mr Monday	35 tons	6 2 6

The shipment of 19 October is the last record of the Southampton Paving Commissioners dealing directly with the Guernsey shippers. John Monday was the Southampton paving contractor and it seems likely that Southampton reverted to the more usual practice elsewhere of paying the pavior for the total paving contract, thus the Guernseymen involved no longer appear in the surviving records.

Of the many thousands of Guernsey granite pebbles imported into England to pave its towns and cities the Southampton record can only account for 4,060 tons - just enough, at 5cwt per square yard, to pave Southampton High Street from Bargate to Watergate; a mere fraction of a once thriving trade. Perhaps the many heaps of pebbles lying on the seabed around Guernsey are all that remain of this important 18th century trade and the ships that carried it.

Pots

The small jar or bottle (Fig. 6) recovered from St Peter Port harbour by Richard Keen and his fellow divers is representative of a type of pottery container that has a wide distribution in the Channel Islands and on the mainland. Its style, fabric, general production technique and distribution all suggest a continental origin either in Normandy or the Loire valley area, but as yet no examples are known from France. They are all in smooth, pinky-buff or buff fine sandy fabric with sparse red and black iron inclusion. Various individual fabric variations are known but the consistent size and style link them together to a single production area.

The Guernsey jar is in a smooth, sandy, buff fabric with sparse black and red iron inclusions. It is finely potted but wide internal throwing grooves and diagonal stress marks at the waist and neck indicate a fast production technique and are generally signs of mass-production. All other examples known show the same internal marks.

Unstratified finds from the seabed are notoriously difficult to date. Fortunately several similar vessels were recovered from two early 18th century contexts in Southampton. In 1965, during the restoration of Watergate, a group of pottery was found in a garderobe shaft contained within a hollow buttress at the west of the surviving structure (Faulkner 1975, Fig.11 and p 9). The group included Verwood and other local wares of the early 18th century and at least four examples of the small jars (Fig. 1-4). The other Southampton example (Fig. 5) came from Pit 1 on the Canutes Palace site excavated in 1959 , (Aberg 1975 p

221), where the pottery was 'predominantly early 18th century.' Similar vessels are known from other coastal sites including Poole, (Bartenetal 1992 p 80 nos. 212, 213, p 81 no. 244, p 117 no 817) and the Isle of Wight (Ryde Middle Bank).

These jars also occur on many inland sites. Seven were found on the Oxford Bodleian Extension site in 1937 , (Mitford 1939 p 139), one of which survives in the Ashmolean Museum (1937, 462). Other Oxford examples come from All Souls College (Ash. Mus. 1921, 236) and 39-41 High Street (Ash. Mus. 1968, 791 & 792). There is another in the Herbert Art Gallery and Museum in Coventry (Shelton Collection) and others are known from Leicester and Northampton.

This distribution pattern, together with their convenient size and relative strength, suggests it was for their contents that the jars were traded, perhaps Guernsey cider or, better still, Calvados. The Southampton finds had a coating of lime-scale which with their find spot on a garderobe gives a good indication of a possible secondary use.

Figure 1

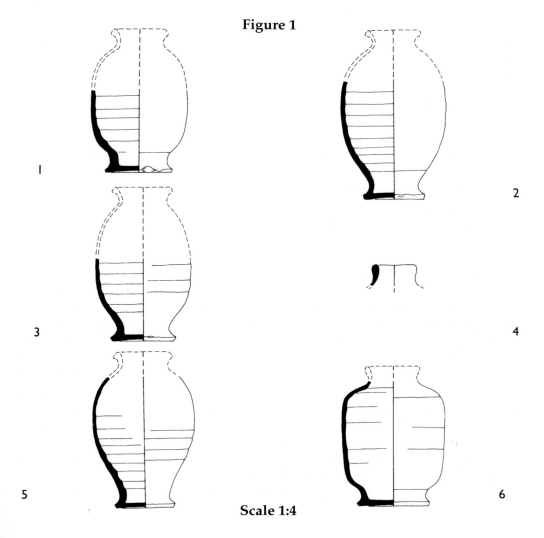

Scale 1:4

Figure 1

1.   Jar; lower body and base. Southampton, Watergate 1964. Pink-buff outer surface and margin and pink inner surface. The smooth clay matrix, slightly micaceous, with abundant fine, well-sorted clear quartz; abundant fine and medium red iron inclusion with some coarser fragments.

2.   Jar; body and base. Southampton, Watergate 1964. Same fabric as No. 1 but slightly reduced externally turning the irons slightly grey.

3.   Jar; lower body and base. Southampton, Watergate 1964. Orange fabric, smooth clay matrix, slightly micaceous, with abundant, well-sorted clear and grey quartz; moderate fine and medium red iron and sparse fine and medium black iron.

4.   Jar rim. Southampton, Watergate 1964. Red-brown throughout. The clay matrix is slightly more sandy than the other samples, with abundant inclusions of fine quartz and red iron.

5.   Jar; lower body and base. Southampton, SOU 126 Pit 1. This has the same fabric as No. 3.

6.   Jar; nearly complete profile; two spots of clear lead glaze on the body. St Peter Port harbour, Guernsey, G2901. Buff-white fabric with a slightly more open clay matrix than the other samples but the same inclusions; abundant fine quartz, not so well-sorted, some medium-sized fragments, moderately abundant red iron which is ill-sorted ranging in size from fine to medium with some coarse fragments. The clay is slightly micaceous.

Bangs

Among the finds from the Vale Castle is a small bronze cannon , (Barton 1984 Fig. 16.14). A similar piece was found in an 18th century context on the West Hall site in Southampton (SOU 110). The Southampton find (below) contained a black powdery residue as did the Vale cannon, which were probably the remains of blank charges. Both guns are bored through to a large tapering touchhole well out of proportion to the bore. Two similar miniature cannon were recovered from an 18th century ship wrecked in Mullion Cove, Cornwall (Mc Bridle 1975p 244). These too '...show evidence of being fired. but would appear much too small for effective signal guns.' However, experiments by the author using a miniature replica steel cannon, a tightly fitting paper wad, very fine Black Powder (Nobel FFFG) and a 6x burning glass produced a most satisfactory bang.

In the National Maritime Museum, Greenwich (NMM ref D325) there is a device known as a 'fixed time-gun dial' with a small bronze cannon fitted to a circular marble base containing a sundial and a burning glass with azimuth adjustment to focus the rays from the sun onto the touchhole. The base is inscribed *Victor Chevalier, Ingr. Brevete quai de a'l'horloge 77 a Paris*. That these devices actually worked is given credence by an article in the Daily Telegraph, (Holmes 1994) where '...in the gardens of the Palais Royal, there is a little brass gun known as *le petit canon*, which was invented by an 18th century clockmaker to fire automatically on the stroke of midday. This ingenious mechanism works by means of a large magnifying glass adjusted to concentrate the rays of sunlight on a powder detonator when the sun is exactly at the zenith.' A recent note in Country Life(Richardson 1995) draws attention to an enterprising Oxfordshire craftsman, one David Harber, who is offering for sale working replicas of the Palais Royal timepiece which was '...originally designed by Arthur Chevalier to inform the gardeners of the noon hour.'

It seems likely that the Vale and Southampton miniature cannon are of French origin and were originally parts of fixed time-gun dials. The traditional reminder of noon with a bang can still be heard from Castle Cornet in Guernsey, but alas no longer sun-powered.

The Palais Royal petit canon carries the inscription, *Horus Non Numero Nisi Serenas* - 'I only count the happy hours,' as I do the many hours I have spent with Burns.

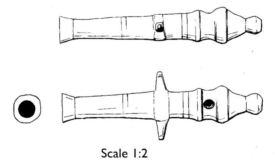

Scale 1:2

Figure 2: Miniature bronze cannon from West Hall, Southampton, SOU 110 F39.

Acknowledgement

Grateful thanks are due to Duncan Brown for the fabric descriptions and encouragement, Maureen Mellor for information on the Oxford jars and Simon Griffin for the drawings.

References

1   Aberg, F. A.   1975   The Excavations, 1959-1961, pp 176-229 in
                                    Platt & Coleman-Smith. (see 12)

2	Barton, K. J.	1984	Excavations at the Vale Castle, Guernsey, *Transactions La Société Guernesiaise*, Vol XXI, pp 485-538.
3	Barton et al	1992	The Catalogue of the Pottery, pp 65-130 in Horsey. (see 7)
4	Davies, J. S.	1883	*A History of Southampton*
5	Faulkner, P.	1975	The surviving medieval buildings, pp 56-124 in Platt & Coleman-Smith. (see 12)
6	Holmes, R.	1994	A letter from Paris, *Daily Telegraph*, October 1, p 8.
7	Horsey, I. P.	1992	Excavations in Poole, 1973-1983. *Dorset Natural History and Archaeological Society* mono series No. 10.
8	Jeffreys, S.	1988	Pebbles, Posts and Purbeck Paving: a study of early 18th century street paving in London. *Trans. Assoc. for Studies in the Conservation of Historic Buildings*, Vol 13, pp 29-41.
9	Lewis, L.	1993	The Paving of Hyde Street, 1773-4. *Winchester Museum Service Newsletter, issue 16*, pp 5-9.
10	McBride, P., Larn, R. & Davis, R.	1975	A mid-17th century merchant ship found near Mullion Cove. *Int. Jour. of Nautical Arch*, Vol 4, pp 237-252.
11	Mitford, R. I.	1939	The Archaeology of the Bodleian Extension, *Oxoniensia, Vol IV*, pp 89-146.
12	Platt, C. & Coleman-Smith, R.	1975	*Excavations in Medieval Southampton, 1953-1969, Vol. 1.*
13	Richardson, T.	1995	Town and Country, *Country Life*, August 17, p 59.
14	Stovold, J.	1990	Minute Book of the Pavement Commission for Southampton, 1770-1789, *Southampton Record Series, Vol. XXXI.*

A Catalogue of the Cliffside Fortifications of Guernsey

BY

MIKE HILL

Introduction

The 1978-80 excavation of the main rampart of the Jerbourg Earthwork above Petit Port, near the Doyle Monument, found the works to be much more complicated and to cover a far longer time-span than was previously assumed (Burns 1988). The substantial, and apparently unrecorded, prehistoric earthwork across Pointe De La Moye was recognised in 1981, and the smaller earthwork on the Jerbourg Promontory near the Peastacks was discovered shortly afterwards. These finds initiated a systematic search of the cliffsides of Guernsey hoping to find more prehistoric works.

Although various works were located, none appeared to be of prehistoric origin. Most of the constructions seem to relate to the more recent age of firearms, mainly cannon. The Victorian gun emplacements are well known. A series of other more obscure sites were found, some amounting to little more than levelled areas of soil, some with stone faced bulwarks, and some utilising the high outcrops of rock.

Three main types of site were found and these seem to relate to differing periods of construction. I have designated these 'Early High Level Rock,' 'Early Low Level.' and 'Victorian' emplacements. Perhaps the three site types are of differing ages and reflect developments in gun efficiency. The fact that a number of 'Victorian' emplacements directly overlook 'Early' sites would seem to support this theory.

It must be stressed that this was a fieldwork study and my interpretation of the sites was made without recourse to history books and with little reference to documentary evidence. Many pre-Victorian features are so basic that in all probability no records were kept of their precise location. One site has been destroyed by vandals, access to others is made dangerous by recent landslips, and the elements erode others. The finds areas of the two prehistoric sites have been monitored on a fairly regular basis up to 1993.

This summary attempts to condense into a more useable form the three volumes of detailed notes, photographs, location and site plans which are archived, together with the finds from some sites, at the Guernsey Museum.

Many of the recent archaeological activities in Guernsey were instigated by Bob Burns and his infectious enthusiasm for the subject. This study was conceived in a trench during the 1975-78 excavations of the Jerbourg Ramparts. Dirt archaeology (active digging) has its drawbacks, often being cold hard work, but jovial banter and the continual exploration of ideas are some of the many rewards. Bob always maintained that archaeology should be enjoyed; field archaeology on the splendid cliffs of Guernsey was a real pleasure for me.

This report was compiled in late 1993 and contained cross references to data archived at the Guernsey Museum. The text of the catalogue is largely unchanged but all the figures have been adapted and the concluding discussion has been added for this paper. Copies of the original document are lodged with both the Guille-Allès and Priaulx Libraries and with La Société Guernesiaise.

Details of Study

Although this study deals with the cliff fortifications, one exception is made by including the fortifications at Albecq on the west coast where the Early and Victorian emplacements can be viewed easily. Château d'Albecq is the most important and complete example of its type in Guernsey. The fine stonework of this built-up outcrop is clearly visible, as is its exposed position and rearguard gully (ditch). The splendid Victorian Burton Battery which supersedes and overlooks the old site should help put into perspective the general pattern of what can be found in the cliffside fortifications.

The main study extends from Fort Pezeries east and north to Fermain Bay, where dense vegetation makes study diffficult.

The format of the catalogue gives site name, parish and map reference and fortification type followed by a brief description of the site. The map references refer to the current OS map.

The three site plans attempt to put these various features on an OS map. It should be remembered that these are solo fieldwork efforts and none of the features has been subjected to a measured survey. Aerial photographs and site visits helped to adapt these maps for archaeological purposes, but the plans are for guidance only.

Summary of Types

Prehistoric
A simple earth rampart, bank and ditch system built to defend a promontory.

Early High Level Rock
Rock outcrops built up and levelled to mount cannon. Cliff-top platforms also used.

Early Low Level
Earth bulwark or rock shield used to front fairly basic emplacement. Both types of early defence usually have some form of rear-guard ditch system.

Victorian

Well engineered defence emplacements, normally placed higher than early sites. No rear-guard ditch.

The Catalogue

Where more detailed information about the various sites is required reference should be made to the original documents. A complete list of sites is given at page 162 and a map showing the location of the sites is on pp. 160-1

1 Rocq Du Guet, Albecq, Catel. WV295 805

Early watch point and Victorian signal with cannon. Strategic observation post. Probably used since early times, through the Victorian period and during WW2.

2 Burton Battery, Albecq, Catel. WV291 805

Victorian cannon emplacement. A well constructed granite platform, mounting four cannon covering Albecq and Cobo sea area.

3 Château d'Albe, Albecq, Catel. WV228 805

Early High Level rock, cannon emplacement. An isolated rock outcrop built up on all sides to form a level platform for cannon. Iron rivets found on site suggest substantial timber lacing to hold clay infill. Site mentioned by name on early maps. A natural sea gully replaces a ditch as a rearguard defence.

4 Fort Pezeries, Pleinmont, Torteval. WV239 763

Early low level and Victorian. A well built fort on a low promontory in a position which covers the approaches to Rocquaine Bay. The emplacement mounted two cannon in 1680 and three guns in the Victorian period.

5 Pleinmont Battery, Pleinmont, Torteval. WV237 761

Early Watch-house and Victorian. Probably the site of the signal/watch point illustrated in the Legge Survey of 1680. The site was named 'Gun upon a High Rock' on Grey's map of 1816. The site mounted one 18 pounder gun.

6 Narrow Point, Pleinmont, Torteval. WV236 760

Victorian cannon platform. A small platform mounting one 9 pounder gun. Breastworks: a number of banks along the edge of the low cliffs are still visible in the area from Pezeries to Narrow Point.

7 Château De La Mouette, Pleinmont Point, Torteval. WV236 756

Early high level rock, cannon emplacement. Forgotten site. A high, isolated rock outcrop below, and joined to the cliff by a narrow causeway. The surviving fragments of stonework suggest that the site was very similar to Château

D'Albe. Iron rivets of identical design were found on the site indicating that a similar form of timber lacing was used to hold the platform infill. The main platform was probably on the NW side, but stonework on the landward side suggests that some form of access was possible to the upper areas on the seaward side, probably through a gap in the outcrop. The seaward side is now bare rock. Traces of stonework indicate that the cannon platform was small and the gun covered a similar field of fire to the Victorian narrow point gun. Recent landslips and cliff-falls have substantially reduced the level area of the landbridge. Access is dangerous. The site is named in the Gardner 1787 survey indicating recent use, but it is not marked as operational. Legge 1680 mentions Fort Pezeries and Fort Pleinmont, but the latter is not marked. It seems probable that Château De La Mouette was part of the Pezeries complex and may in fact be Fort Pleinmont.

8 Pleinmont Watch-House, Torteval. WV242 753 Victorian.

9 Mont Herault Watch-House, St. Pierre du Bois. WV250 750 Victorian.

10 (Belle Elizabeth) Le Long Cavaleux, St Pierre Du Bois. WV254 750
Possible Early Low Level defence work. A complex cliff-side slope area with many features, most of which were probably associated with farming activities, some continuing until the 1900s. A substantial stone walled bulwark across a narrow gully, was possibly a defence work; but it's real purpose is far from obvious. A sunken area behind a wall/bank at the cliff-edge may be a breastwork; but agricultural use seems more likely.

11 Le Long Cavaleux, St Pierre Du Bois. WV258 751
Early Low Level - Platform/Barrier. A short section of stone wall on cliff-edge above the sheer drop of the landbridge to the low promontory. The purpose of such an isolated fragment of the wall is not clear. Vandals systematically destroyed the wall in 1987-89. This action revealed some massive foundation stones and rubble infill, suggesting a military use of the site. The landbridge over the natural arch has a gully cut across it; this seems to be a modified natural feature. The wall on the landward side of the gully would allow the ground level to be raised on the SE side, and thereby form an effective barrier some 3m in height, to prevent a landing from seaward. A very similar feature exists at the St Clair's Battery at Petit Bôt. The site seems to be of early origin and may possibly have served also as a low platform for a small gun.

12 Les Tielles Watch-House And Battery, Torteval. WV263 749
Victorian. The site of the watch-house on the high ground is still evident. The gun platform lower down the slope mounted two 18 pounder guns. Re-use during WW2 has resulted in alterations to the platform and bulwark.

13 Le Prevoté, St Pierre Du Bois. WV278 746

Victorian site of watch-house and signal post. Now has a German WW2 observation tower built on the site, but some original walling is still visible.

14 La Corbiere (Corbiere Castle), Forest.   WV282 743

Possibly prehistoric; probably very early and early high level rock. The promontory is isolated by a bank and ditch system across the narrowest point between sheer cliff faces. The interpretation of this site is extremely difficult and it is essential that the plan on Fig 1 (p.163) is consulted. Furze fires in the late 70s and early 80s laid the surface bare. Field work took place a few years after when vegetation had started to recover. During many hours on the site very few finds were located; a total absence of pottery, very little flint. Modern material was mainly glass and WW2 Machine Gun Bullets. The main features that can be summarised are:-

A. The Bank and Ditch system: A main rampart with one smaller bank and two ditches; a later boundary wall runs through the outer ditch. These banks and ditches have not been dated; if of prehistoric origin, the sharp profile suggests a later re-cut.

B. The Summit area: A WW2 bunker and other smaller works were constructed by German Forces. These probably erased some features; however, the damage is possibly not as great as it appears. The WW2 works are clearly defined and it is still possible with a little imagination to trace the earlier basic outline depicted on the1680 Legge Survey. A print of 1680 showing the 'Castle' in ruins indicates the summit was open ground.

C. The West Quarries: The west side of the summit appears to have been extensively quarried for poor quality stone or gravel. A track runs over the boundary wall and ditches and then up the main rampart. The track seems to have given access to the quarry workings before being diverted, at a later date, to give access to the lower areas of the promontory. A crude wall was built along the area below the quarry workings. The WW2 works behind the wall, and the communication trenches, seem to have caused very little damage to this area.

D. The Stub-Wall on West End of the Main Rampart: This feature is apparently visible on the 1680 print. The remains of a wall clearly show in the cliff-edge section and are set in a low bank linked to the main rampart. A 90 degree north/south alignment joins the rampart higher up - as indicated on the 1680 plan and print.

E. Lower West Slope Area: The later alignment of the track ends near several alignments of stones, which form crude terracing. Below these runs what appears to be a breastwork aligned with the cliff edge.This work commands Havre De La Bon Repos beach and cliffside track and seems to be pre-WW2.

F. Lower South Slope Features: The track ends above a path giving access to sea-rocks used by fishermen. Various stone alignments, dug-out areas, wall footings and paths have been identified in this general area.

G. Lower South Face Area: Two substantial walls were built between gaps in the outcrops above sheer cliff, and filled with rubble. Stone wall footings run across the lower face area, but these seem to have little strength or obvious function. The two infilled areas were possibly early cannon platforms and the walls may have held levelling material for pathways to them. One of these pathways may have run across the lower area and linked up with the west track; it is now cut by WW2 spoil from the main bunker.

H. East Coast Terracing: Four or five alignments of stones and a crudely constructed wall form a series of terraces. Their function is not clear. Some stones are huge; the effort needed to move them seems incompatible with an agricultural use for this area. The area commands the landing gully below suggesting a possible defensive role for the terraces. A similar plain slope above this area is not terraced, which may be significant.

I. East Bank and Rampart: Some WW2 overburden rubble covers the central entrance track and also part fills both ditches. A track seems to lead to two WW2 machine-guns posts. However, as stated earlier the main alignments of the summit seem undamaged.

J. Central Access Track: A slice appears to have been removed from the edge of the main rampart to improve access. Some iron rivets were found embedded in the track in 1993. They appeared to be in or associated with the original soil. However, although six rivets were identical to those found on Château D'Albecq and Château De La Mouette suggesting a similar fortification age, the rivets were associated with some later WW2 material. Therefore, although the rivets were close to where some form of gate may have existed, they could have been re-deposited spoil material from the 1920 excavation by Lukis.

15 Pointe De La Moye, Forest. WV297 742
Prehistoric Earthwork Promontory Fort and Early Low Level. (Fig 2 p.164) A major promontory defended by a substantial main rampart and one or two smaller banks with ditches across the narrowest point; combined with the sheer sea cliffs on either side form an effective defence work. The following points are relevant.

A. The main rampart is massive, was probably stone faced, and has the entrance ramp on the east side a third of the way down.

B. It is possible that the entrance stonework is visible, but the track was also used in more recent years for an access way to the harbour. This path zigzags down the east slope. The secondary bank and ditch system is complicated and needs more study; the east and west sides probably differ.

C. There appears to be a single secondary bank, two quarry ditches and the drop to the first ditch forming an initial pseudo bank. An old track leading to the harbour zigzags down the east side between the two banks and cuts through the end of the main rampart.

D. A later track cuts through the rampart higher up, and now carries the footpath. The occupation areas were probably on the east side.

E. A large open area is situated behind the rampart and entrance. The steeper slope further south seems to have had more level areas cut into it, possibly for occupation purposes.

F. Some possible scarping is visible on the south end.

G. The prehistoric works seem to rely on the natural defence provided by the outcrop to a large degree. A crude platform on the southern tip seems to be an early low level cannon emplacement.

H. The prehistoric site has not been dated, and only a single plain sherd of pottery has been recovered during the recent studies.

16 Les Sommeilleuses Watch-House and Magazine, Forest. WV300747
Victorian

17 St Clairs Battery Petit Bôt, Forest. WV304749
Possible early low level platform and Victorian. The site now holds a substantial Victorian gun emplacement which mounted the two 24 pounder cannon. The bulwark was modified during WW2 to take a machine gun nest. The bulwark appears to have been strengthened at some stage by adding a wall to the front of an existing bulwark wall. An existing natural gully seems to have been modified to form a deeper defensive ditch in front of the platform. A sunken area at the east end of this lower gully/ditch suggests that an earlier low level gun platform may have existed on the site prior to the Victorian works. The magazine for the later battery is situated in the valley a short distance away. A series of breastworks were constructed along the cliff edge and are marked in Gardner 1787. Some of these were found during the recent fieldwork.

18 Mount Hubert Platform, St Martin. WV308 759

Early High Level platform. This site is marked in Gardner 1787. The platform now exists as a level area on the highest part of the coastal footpath. Traces of the bulwark stonework are also visible.

19 Icart Battery, St Martin. WV316 745

Victorian. This emplacement mounted one 24 pounder gun and can be found amongst the scrub low on the cliff-slope near the edge.

20 Château D'Icart, St Martin. WV318 741

Early High Level Rock/Victorian. This substantial rock promontory is isolated from the cliff by a very narrow ridge (now unsafe). The summit has clearly been levelled, and traces of stonework around the top suggest that it was once surrounded by a low wall to hold the levelling clay infill. Perhaps the west gully was also infilled. The site could have mounted two guns. A depression on the lower level adjacent to the causeway suggests a guard-house. The track along the low east side is supported by stonework and may lead to a third platform facing east or south-east. The rock outcrop of the access causeway has clearly been worked to improve the path. On the point is a Victorian Watch-house Signal Station-a ruin in undergrowth scrub near the coastal path.

21 Saints Bay - Right, Saint Martin. WV322 745

Early Low Level/Victorian. A sunken area behind a substantial earthen bulwark on the west side of the bay. This emplacement clearly has the same purpose as the Victorian site overlooking it. Some breast works are visible through the scrub. On the east side two breast works were located. Both seem to have had WW2 re-use. Other work shown in the Gardner 1787 survey were not located. The Victorian emplacement mounted two 24 pounder guns, and the magazine is at the back of the site.

22 Saints Bay - Left Battery, St Martin. WV322 748

This Victorian battery was vaguely detectable in dense vegetation.

23 Bon Port Platform, St Martin. WV325 748

Early Low Level emplacement. Forgotten site. A 10m x 8m levelled area of soil behind a natural rock outcrop/bulwark. The top of the outcrop has had higher peaks of rock removed to improve the field of fire.

24 Moulin Huet Right , St Martin. WVV327 750

Early High Level platform/Victorian. Forgotten site. This platform is marked on the 1787 map. The site is now occupied by a seat which is next to the cliff path. The outline of the platform is clearly visible and some original stonework survives. The site is directly above the Victorian Moulin Huet right battery. A fine flagstone platform behind a walled, and outcrop, bulwark. A crude magazine is set in the cliff. WW2 works levelled the west bulwark and installed a machine gun post.

25 Moulin Huet Left Battery and Watch-house, St Martin. WV328 752

Victorian gun platform. The supposed site of this platform is hidden by scrub. It was not visited. The ruins of the watch-house is visible.

26 Petit Port, St Martin. WV

Two level areas are visible from the cliff path. These may be early platform sites. Both overlook the bay.

27 Jerbourg: Main Earthwork - West Side, St Martin. WV338 752

Prehistoric and multi period earthwork. The construction chronology of these massive defensive earthen ramparts were determined by excavation (Burns 1988). On the west side of the site two beehive huts were clearly shown by Carey Curtis (1923), but recent searches failed to locate the lower hut. The upper hut was probably destroyed during WW2; but a circular depression near WW2 works could be its site. The main rampart is impressively scarped and massive when viewed from the first ditch near the top. Half-way down the slope it becomes a substantial bank. The first ditch is fairly narrow above the sea-cliff and broadens towards the top. Quite a large open area separates these features from the outer bank and two ditches, which only descend to the valley stream. The sharp profile of the latter features suggests a later construction date. A number of cuttings and other features were located. A stone-lined structure is set in the upper horn-work below the Doyle Column car park. This crescent shaped feature is protected by an earth bank. It may be a later feature associated with farming activities.

28 Cannon Rock, St Martin. WV335 748

Early High Level rock, cannon emplacement. The classic example of its type. A high outcrop of rock was isolated from the cliff by a ditch cut across the narrow neck of land joining it to the cliffside. The summit area was built up with stone infill, probably held by timber lacing, and the bulwark was surrounded by a stone wall. The gun was in a central depression and the higher peaks of the outcrop were removed to give a clear field of fire. The site covers the approach to Petit Port and the Moulin Huet sea area. The Bon Port lower level platform effectively covers the other side of the bay. A low bank on the lower level may be part of the defence, and a levelled area on the north side has traces of stonework on its western side and a supporting wall at its northern end. This may be another low level gun platform or the site of a building. There are a number of boundary walls hidden in the scrub on the cliffside. Two features may be associated with the defence works, possibly breastworks, but this is unclear.

29 La Moye Battery, St Martin. WV336 745.
Victorian. A single 24 pounder gun was mounted on this platform. A stone-faced bulwark, with what appears to be a small dug-out magazine, is at the back of the north side. Access to this area of the cliff between Cannon Rock and La Moye Battery is extremely difficult. Boundary walls and other possible defence works are visible.

30 Jerbourg Point, St Martin. WV335 743
Prehistoric earthwork promontory fort. A bank and ditch system across the narrow landbridge which joins the promontory to the main cliffside forms the main defence (fig. 3 p.165). The substantial main rampart runs up the east side to the rocky ridge. The principal points to note are:-

A. The central part of this was built up with a stone faced bank. The west corner was also built up in places but makes more use of the natural rock barrier.

B. The high central part probably acted as the main fighting platform.

C. A high ridge path exists but no entrance way has been identified, although it was probably on the east side. The initial ditch and banks, though more clearly defined on the east side, are now fairly indistinct features.

D. The initial works on the west side are very difficult to locate and may not have existed due to the steep slope on this side. The first ditch has clearly been re-cut and widened at a later date, possibly around 1607 when permission was granted to use the promontory as a rabbit warren.

E and F. Two areas of occupation have been identified on the east side, and it is probable that the large west slope was also used.

G. A variety of prehistoric pottery has been recovered; the age of this is the subject of debate, but may be late Bronze Age to early Iron Age. No excavation has taken place.

31 St Martin's Point Earthwork, St Martin. WV342 748
Prehistoric? A large ditch cut across the promontory. The ditch seems to have an unusual reverse profile and slopes towards the sea.

32 Jerbourg Battery, St Martin. WV342 749
Victorian. A large platform situated in scrub half way up the cliff slope. It mounted two 24 pounder guns. Possibly WW2 works also.

33 Mont Au Nord Battery, St Martin. WV343 749

Early Low Level. This battery is situated on a low promontory. The earthwork bulwark probably had a stone wall on the inside and five or six gun platforms were stone flagged and the settings are still visible. An open area behind the gun appears to have had a building constructed on the south side. The outline and stone alignments are still visible. A low path on the north side leads to a hollow area behind the inner defence bank, possibly another building site. Set in the modern main path are a large number of small stones. These lead up to an outcrop of rock and also north along the edge of the hollow area, suggesting some form of wall was built. The outcrop has a gap cut in it, and this was obviously used to guard the approach to the site. The original entrance appears to have been more to the south. Two of the defence banks were recently cut back for the current path. After the initial cliff drop to the first deep ditch there are two substantial rear defence banks and another ditch. The first ditch was deepened at a later stage by a secondary cut, which may be contemporary with a breastwork on the cliff edge above the site.

34 Divette Landing, Jerbourg, St Martin. WV341 754

Several small promontories seem to have had small defensive ditches cut across them, the largest being just south of the breakwater of the landings. The landing area is well known and its four worked stone mooring bollards can still be seen. There are a number of boundary walls, banks and tracks in the area.

35 Bec Du Nez Battery, St Martin. WV341 756

Victorian. Three 12 pounder cannon were mounted on this emplacement, which has a magazine/guardroom concealed at the rear of the site. A levelled area above the site may have been from earlier works.

36 Fermain - South.

Early low level. Two breastworks, La Ricou and Le Grand Creux, were located along the south cliff. The latter could have mounted a gun. The south magazine or the gun site (Gardner 1787) were found.

37 Fermain Bay.

The south battery platform, still paved, is visible from the cliff-path. Access to the high north platform is not possible. The tower is still preserved near the tea room.

38 Becquet Battery and Magazine.

These were located high on the cliff but the lower platform could not be found, nor could a site in Gardner 1787 on the north cliff overlooking the bay.

Discussion

Prehistoric

The most significant discovery was the massive and complex Pointe de la Moye earthwork. Some future excavation may date the site accurately to enable its place in the prehistoric defences of the island to be worked out. The smaller, but not insignificant, Jerbourg Point earthwork appears to date from the Late Bronze or Early Iron Age, approximately 800-500 BC (Cunliffe pers. comm.). The site may have been in use during a period when the main Jerbourg earthwork was abandoned for some reason. Much study remains to be undertaken before the chronology of these Iron Age fortifications can be established accurately, particularly in an island-wide context.

Early - High Level Rock

La Corbiere is a major promontory which has been subjected to some form of fortification. While it is possible that the earthworks are prehistoric, I suspect they are not, although the site has probably been used in a defensive context since very early times. The exact nature of any fortification seems elusive. The print from Legge 1680 Report which shows the Castle in ruins adds mystery to the puzzle. In my view the iron rivets found on the site are highly significant and conclusively link one phase of activity at La Corbiere with the early high-level cannon sites of Château D'Albe on the west coast and the important cliff site of Château de la Mouette. The fact that there appear to be two crude platforms at La Corbiere would seem to add weight to this theory.

La Corbiere seems to have escaped much historical reference, but one note states that the defence was commanded from above and was therefore considered to be obsolete (Danby report). This statement would seem to indicate an early use of the site. The recent fieldwork has found the defended high-level rock defence to be a distinct fortification type on Guernsey, the most important cliffs sites being Château de la Mouette, La Corbiere, Château D'Icart and the Cannon Rock at Jerbourg. I suspect that all these sites are of a similar age and that they were part of a chain of emplacements covering the various anchorages, bays and landings along the cliffs. The size of the works at La Corbiere and its central position suggests the site may have had some considerable overall value in the early cliffside defence network.

Early - Low Level

It was not possible for the early engineers to defend all potential landing sites with the high-level rock type emplacements. Therefore a series of distinct low-level sites were constructed. Most of these used either rock outcrops as shields or single earthen bulwarks to shelter the cannon site. Many of these emplacements vary; however the height above sea-level seems to be a common factor, and they appear to fit neatly into the early defence system. Examples of this form of defence work can be found at, Le Long Cavaleux, La Point de la Moye, possibly at St Clair's Battery, Saints West and Bon Port.

Other Early Sites

Fort Pezeries has a long history as a defence work and the near by Pleinmont Battery appears to have been used as a signal station in early times. The multi-gun Mont au Nord battery was a very well defended low-level promontory site which appears to have early origins. The pre-Victorian sites which deserve mention are the Mont Hubert and Moulin Huet platforms, both of which were marked in Gardner 1787 but are unusual in that the guns were situated on cliff-top platforms.

Victorian Sites

The construction and siting of the Victorian emplacements was superior to the early sites, although most commanded similar fields of fire. More attention seems to have been paid to defending potential landing bays, but in all probability some earlier sites covering these areas were erased during the upgrading process. Many of the Victorian sites were modified and used during WW2 by German forces.

Acknowledgements

Thanks are due to H. M. Greffier for permission to view the 1680 Legge Survey report. Bob Burns kindly offered constructive comment on the various drafts of this paper. The assistance of both the Guernsey Museum and the Priaulx Library personnel, as well as various other individuals is also gratefully acknowledged.

References

Burns, R.B., 1988: Excavations at Jerbourg, Guernsey. *Guernsey Museum Monog. No 1.*

Burns, R.B., Cunliffe, B. & Sebire, H. 1996: Guernsey, an Island Community of the Atlantic Iron Age. *Guernsey Museum Monog. No 6.*

Carey, Curtis, 1923: Jerbourg Fortifications. *Transactions, La Société Guernesiaise.* Vol 9 pp 158-160

Danby Earl,1631: Military report on Guernsey defences.

Gardner, 1787: The Survey of Guernsey for the Duke of Richmond.

Legge, 1680: Military survey of Guernsey.

Lukis, 1932: Report of excavations at La Corbiere. *Transactions, La Société Guernesiaise.* Vol XI, p. 277.

SITE NAMES FOR MAP

1   Rocq Du Guet .... Early, Victorian
2   Burton Battery .... Victorian
3   Château D'Albe, Albecq .... Early high level rock
4   Fort Pezeries .... Early low level, Victorian
5   Pleinmont Battery .... Early, Victorian
6   Narrow Point.. Victorian
7   Château De La Mouette, Pleinmont Point .... Early high level rock
8   Pleinmont Watch-House .... Victorian
9   Mont Herault Watch-House .... Victorian
10 Le Long Cavaleux (Belle Elizabeth) .... Early low level
11 Le Long Cavaleux .... Early low level
12 Les Tielles Watch House and Battery .... Victorian
13 Le Prevote .... Victorian
14 La Corbiere .... Prehistoric, Early,
    Early high level rock
15 Pointe De La Moye .... Prehistoric, Early low
    .... level
16 Les Sommeilleuses Watch-House and Magazine Victorian
17 St Clairs Battery .... Early, low level Victorian
18 Mount Hubert Platform .... Early, high level rock
19 Icart Battery .... Victorian
20 Château D'Icart .... Early high level rock,
    Victorian
21 Saints Bay - Right Battery .... Early low level, Victorian
22 Saints Bay - Left Battery.................................... Victorian
23 Bon Port Platform .... Early low level
24 Moulin Huet - Right .... Early high level, Victorian
25 Moulin Huet Left Battery .... Victorian
26 Petit Port .... ? Early high level
27 Jerbourg Main Earthworks.................................. Prehistoric, mutli period
28 Cannon Rock .... Early high level rock
29 La Moye Battery.. Victorian
30 Jerbourg Point .... Prehistoric
31 St Martin's Point Earthworks .... Prehistoric
32 Jerbourg Battery .... Victorian
33 Mont Au Nord Battery .... Early low level
34 Divette Landing .... Early low level
35 Bec Du Nez Battery .... Victorian
36 Fermain - South.. Early low level, Victorian
37 Fermain Bay .... Victorian
38 Becquet Battery and Magazine .... Victorian

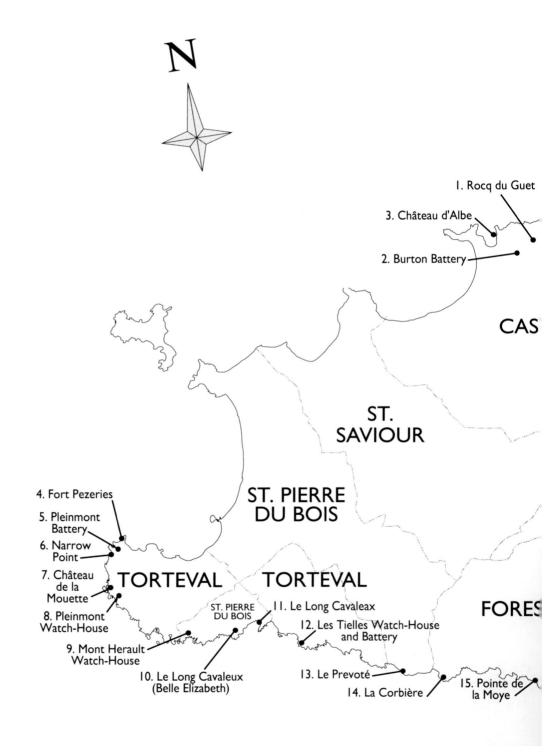

N

1. Rocq du Guet

3. Château d'Albe

2. Burton Battery

CAS

ST.
SAVIOUR

ST. PIERRE
DU BOIS

4. Fort Pezeries

5. Pleinmont
Battery

6. Narrow
Point

7. Château
de la
Mouette

8. Pleinmont
Watch-House

9. Mont Herault
Watch-House

10. Le Long Cavaleux
(Belle Elizabeth)

TORTEVAL

TORTEVAL

ST. PIERRE
DU BOIS

11. Le Long Cavaleax

12. Les Tielles Watch-House
and Battery

13. Le Prevoté

14. La Corbière

15. Pointe de
la Moye

FORES

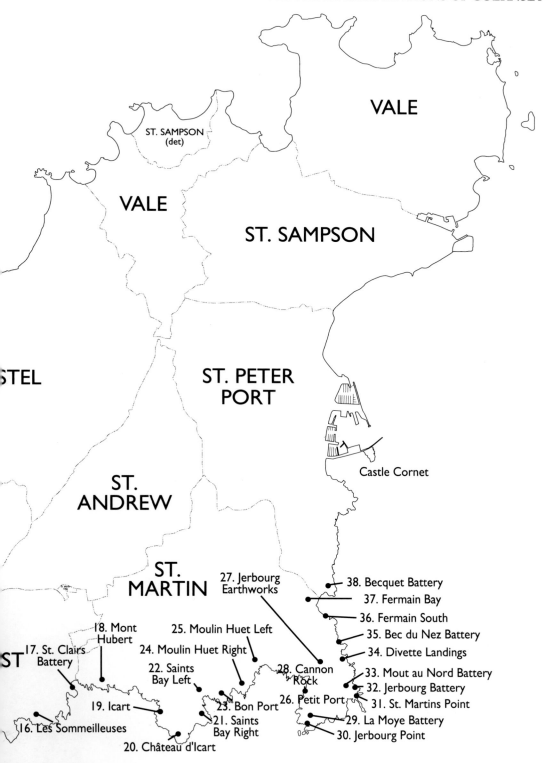

VALE

ST. SAMPSON
(det)

VALE

ST. SAMPSON

ST. PETER
PORT

Castle Cornet

ST.
ANDREW

ST.
MARTIN

27. Jerbourg
Earthworks

38. Becquet Battery

37. Fermain Bay

36. Fermain South

35. Bec du Nez Battery

34. Divette Landings

33. Mout au Nord Battery

32. Jerbourg Battery

31. St. Martins Point

29. La Moye Battery

30. Jerbourg Point

18. Mont
Hubert

25. Moulin Huet Left

24. Moulin Huet Right

22. Saints
Bay Left

28. Cannon
Rock

26. Petit Port

17. St. Clairs
Battery

19. Icart

23. Bon Port

21. Saints
Bay Right

16. Les Sommeilleuses

20. Château d'Icart

STEL

ST

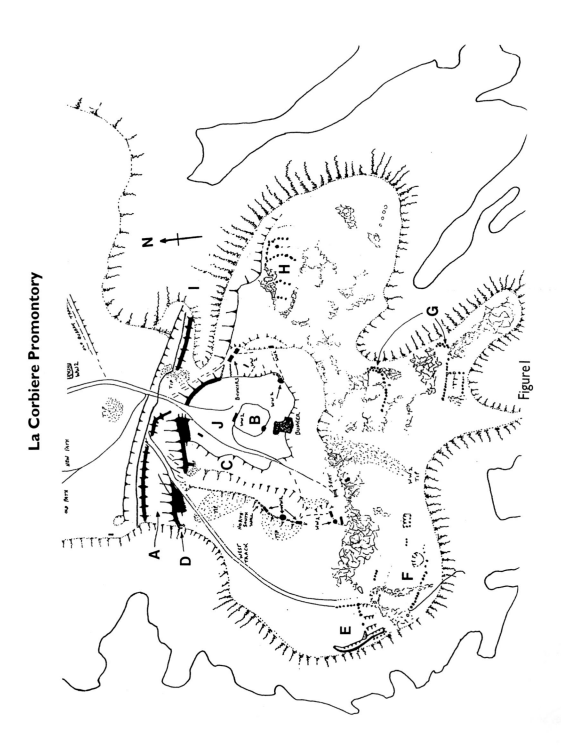

La Corbiere Promontory

Figure1

Pointe de la Moye

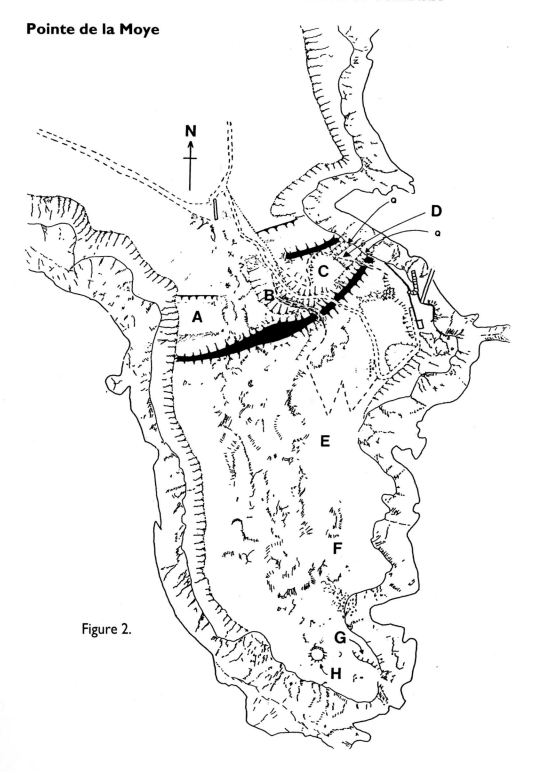

Figure 2.

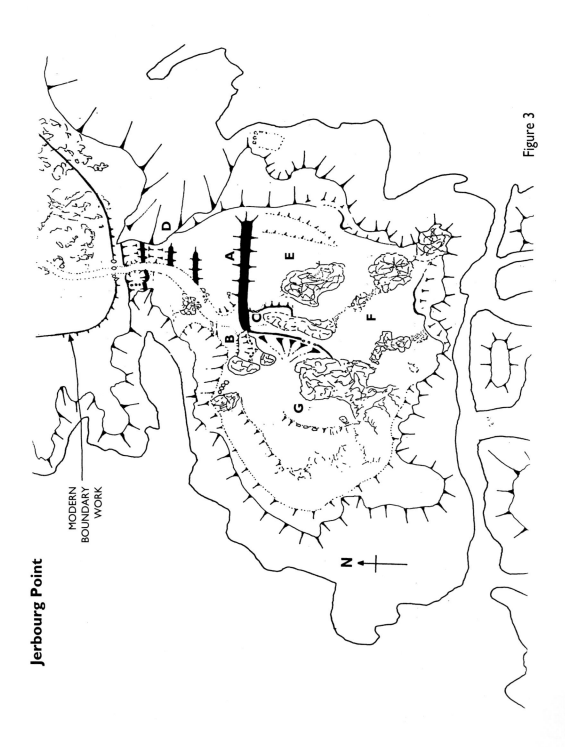

Jerbourg Point

MODERN
BOUNDARY
WORK

N

Figure 3

An Archaeological Bibliography for Guernsey

This bibliography has been compliled to guide researchers to the main texts to date. References to notes etc. have not been included.

Allen, D.F. 1971: The Sark Hoard. *Archaeologia* 103, pp 1-31.

Anon. 1901 Note of the monthly meeting held November 20th, 1901. *Trans Soc. Guernesiaise* Vol V, p 59

Ayscough, F. 1932 Guernsey megaliths: their secrets revealed at night. *Trans. Soc. Guernesiaise II*, Vol XI, pp 365 - 76.

Barton, K. J. 1980 Excavations at Château Des Marais. *Trans. Soc. Guernesiaise* Vol XX, pp 657-702.

Barton, K.J. 1984 Excavations at the Vale Castle, Guernsey, Channel Islands. *Trans. Soc., Guernesiaise.* Vol XXI, pp 485-538

Brett, C.E.B. Buildings in the Town and Parish of St Peter Port *National Trust of Guernsey* 1975

Burns, R. B. 1976 Excavations at the Bordage, St Peter Port. *Trans. Soc. Guernesiaise* Vol XIX, pp 539-553

Burns, R.B. 1976 Pottery from the Saintonge, St Peter Port, Guernsey. *Trans. Soc. Guernesiaise* Vol XX, pp 19-22

Burns, R.B. 1977 The Late Iron Age Site at The Tranquesous, St Saviours, Guernsey. *Trans. Soc. Guernesiaise* Vol XX, pp 118-228.

Burns R.B. 1978 The Contents of a Late 18th Century pit at Candie Road, St Peter Port, Guernsey. *Review of the Guernsey Society.*

Burns R.B. 1978 Medieval and Post-Medieval finds from Forest Lane, St Peter Port, Guernsey *Trans. Soc. Guernesiaise* Vol XX, pp 296-302

Burns, R.B. 1979 An Early Ceramic group from Hauteville, St Peter Port . *Trans. Soc. Guernesiaise* Vol XX, p 441-449

Burns, R.B. 1984 The Prehistoric Pottery in K.J.Barton Excavations at the Vale, Castle, Guernsey *Trans. Soc. Guernesiaise* . Vol XXI, pp 510-512

Burns R.B. and Burns A.G. 1985 Gallo-Roman Finds from Guernsey and Herm. *Trans. Soc. Guernesiaise* Vol XXI, pp 652-666

Burns, R.B. and Kinnes I.A. 1981 The Channel Islands Archaeology and Early History, in *The Blue Guide to the Channel Islands* London pp 2-26.

Burns R.B 1986. Recent work on the Iron Age and Gallo-Roman period in the Bailiwick of Guernsey in *The Archaeology of the Channel Islands* ed. Peter Johnson. Phillimore, Chichester.

Burns R.B. 1987 L'Epoque gallo-romaine un Nouveau Chapitre de L'Histoire de Guernsey in *S.F.E.C.A.G. Actes du Congres de Caen.*

Burns R.B. 1988 Excavations at Jerbourg, Guernsey. *Guernsey Museum Monograph No 1*

Burns R.B. & Batt M. 1990 Excavations at Grandes Rocques, Guernsey. *Revue Archaeologique de L'Ouest de France.*

Burns R.B. 1991 Post-Medieval Normandy stonewares from Guernsey. in Lewis E. ed *Customs and ceramics: Essays presented to Kenneth Barton*, APE Wickham.

Burns R.B. 1993: Warrior burials in Guernsey. *Les Celtes en Normandie.* Revue Archeologique de l' Ouest Suppl. 6 pp 165-71.

Burns R.B. Cunliffe B.W. and Sebire H.R. 1996 Guernsey: An Island Community of the Atlantic Iron Age, *Oxford University Monograph No 46/ Guernsey Museum Monograph No 6.* Oxford

Burns R.B. and Sebire H.R. 1995 A 15th Century Pottery Bank from Guernsey. *Trans. Soc. Guernesiaise* Vol XXIV pp 973-975

Carey, J.J. 1894 *Trans. Soc. Guernesiaise* Vol II pp 333-37

Collum, V.C.C. 1933 Re-excavation of the Déhus Chambered Mound at Paradis, Vale, Guernsey. *Trans. Soc. Guernesiaise.* Vol II p 7.

Curtis S.C. 1912 An account of the discovery and examination of a cist or dolmen of a type novel to Guernsey. *Trans. Soc., Guernesiaise* Vol VI, pp 400-14.

Curtis S.C. 1935 Report of the Antiquarian section, *Trans. Soc. Guernesiaise* Vol XII, pp 256-62.

De Guérin T.W.M. 1910 Our Statue -menhirs and those of France and Italy, *Trans. Soc. Guernesiaise* Vol VI, pp 177-87.

De Guérin T.W.M. 1915 Examination of mound of dolmen of Déhus, Vale October 1915, *Trans Soc., Guernesiaise* Vol VII, pp 191-192.

De Guérin T.W.M. 1915 Examination of mound of dolmen of Le Creux des Fées, *Trans. Soc., Guernesiaise* Vol VII, pp 192-93.

De Guérin T.W.M. 1916 Report on the discovery of two cists on the beach near Rousse Tower, *Trans. Soc., Guernesiaise* Vol VII, pp 328-30.

De Guérin T.W.M. 1917 Sculpture lines on the capstone of the dolmen of Déhus *Trans. Soc. Guernesiaise* Vol VIII, pp 53-54.

De Guérin T.W.M. 1918 Evidence of man in Guernsey during the Bronze Age and early Iron Age. *Trans. Soc. Guernesiaise* VIII, pp 127-41.

De Guérin T.W.M. 1919 Notes on the recent discovery of a human figure sculptured on the dolmen of Déhus, Guernsey, *Trans. Soc. Guernesiaise* Vol VIII, pp 214-21.

De Guérin T.W.M. 1921 List of Dolmens Menhirs and Sacred Rocks. *Trans. Soc. Guernesiaise* Vol IX, pp 30-64.

De Guérin T.W.M. 1925 The megalithic culture of Guernsey. *Trans. Soc. Guernesiaise* Vol IX, pp 456-81.

Derrick G.T. 1906 Archaeological Remains in Guernsey. *Trans. Soc. Guernesiaise* Vol V, pp 229-30.

De Jersey P. 1993 The Early Chronology of Alet and its implications for Hengistbury Head and Cross-Chanel Trade in the Late Iron Age. *Oxford Journal of Archaeology 12*, pp 321-335.

De Jersey P. 1994 *The Archaeology of coinage in Iron Age Armorica.* OUCA.

Girard P. 1981 Summary report on the excavations at Cobo in 1968. *Trans. Soc. Guernesiaise* Vol XXI, pp 94-98

Gosselin, J. 1811 An account of some Druidical remains in the island of Guernsey. *Archaeologia* 117 pp 254-56.

Hill M. 1990 The excavation at La Hougue Catelain, 1982 and 1983 in *Trans. Soc. Guernesiaise*. Vol.XXIII, pp 827-870

Jee, N. 1958 : Archaeological Report *Trans. Soc. Guernesiaise* Vol XVI, p 313.

Johnson, P. ed. 1986 *The Archaeology of the Channel Islands*. Phillimore, Chichester.

Keen R. and Keen, J. 1979 *Information Sheet No.1* Private Publication.

Keen R., 1986. A Review of Roman material from the sea off Guernsey 1860-1980. in *The Archaeology of the Channel Islands*. P. Johnson pp 138-141

Kendrick, T.D. 1928: *The Archaeology of the Channel Islands. Vol, 1. : The Bailiwick of Guernsey* London.

Kinnes, IA. and Grant J.A. 1983 Les Fouaillages and the Megalithic Monuments of Guernsey. *Ampersand.* Alderney.

Kinnes, I.A. 1980 The art of the exceptional: the statue - menhirs of Guernsey in context. *Archaeologia Atlantica*, pp 39-33.

Kinnes I.A. 1982b Les Fouaillages and Megalithic Origins, *Antiquity 56*.

Kinnes I.A. 1986 Les Neolithisation de Iles Anglo-Normandes, *Revue Archaeologique de L'Ouest Supplement* no pp 19-12.

Kinnes, I.A. 1988 Megaliths in Action:some aspects of the Neolithic period in the Channel Islands, *Archaeological Journal*, pp 145 13-59.

Kinnes I.A. and Hibbs J.L. 1989 Le Gardien du tombeau : further reflections on the initial neolithic, *Oxford Journal of Archaeology, 8*, pp 159-166.

Kinnes I.A. 1995 Statue-Menhirs and allied representations in Northern France and the Channel Islands. *Notizie Archeologiche Bergomensi* 3.pp 131-141.

Lukis, F.C. 1844 Observations on the Primaeval Antiquities of the Channel Islands: *Archaeological Journal* 1 pp 144 & 222.

Lukis, F.C. 1845-6 On the Cromlech of Du Tus. *Journal of the British Archaeological Association* 1 p 25.

Lukis, F.C. 1845-6   On Sepulchral Graves in Guernsey. *Journal of the British Archaeological Association* 1 p 305.

Lukis, F.C. 1847 On Stone Celts found in the Channel Islands. *Journal of the British Archaeological Association* 111 p.127.

Lukis, F.C. 1847 On the Cromlech of L'Ancresse Common. *Journal of the British Archaeological Association* 111 p.342.

Lukis, F.C. 1848-9 On the Sepulchral Character of Cromlechs in the Channel Islands. *Journal of British Archaeological Association* IV p.323

Lukis, F.C. 1850 Communication on Hand-Bricks. *Archaeological Journal* VII p.175.

Lukis, F.C. 1853 On a sepulchral Cave found in Guernsey. *Journal of the British Archaeological Society VIII* 64

Lukis F.C. 1854 On the Maenhir. *Journal of British Archaeological Association* IX p. 426

Lukis F.C. 1847 On the Antiquities of Alderney. *Journal of the British Archaeological Association* III p. 127.

Lukis F.C. 1850 Collectanea Antiqua. Unpublished Mss held at Guernsey Museum.

Lukis F.C. 1846 Observations on the Celtic Megaliths: *Archaeologia XXXV* p. 232.

Gosselin, J. 1811 An Account of some Druidicial remains in the island of Guernsey. *Archaeologia XVII* p 254.

Machon, N. 1981 Mysterious Mound. *Guernsey Press*

Monaghan, J. 1987 Decouvertes maritimes provenant du baillage de Guernsey. *SFECAG Actes du congres du Caen* pp 39-44.

Monaghan J., 1988 *The Guernsey Maritime Trust Gazetteer*, 1984-88 Vol XXII 3, pp 453-465.

Monaghan J. 1991 Pottery from Marine Sites around Guernsey. *Journal Rom. Pottery Studies* pp 363-69.

Monaghan J. & Rule M. 1990 A Gallo-Roman Trading Vessel from Guernsey. *Guernsey Museum Monograph No. 5*

Oliver R.A. 1870 Report on the Present State and Condition of Prehistoric Remains in the Channel Islands. *Journal of the Ethnographical Society of London, N.S.* 11 p 45.

Oliver R.A. 1870 (April) Megalithic Structures of the Channel Islands. Their History and Analogues *Quarterly Journal of Science* Vol XXVI p 149.

Renouf. J. and Urry J. 1976 *The First Farmers in the Channel Islands.* Jersey Education Committee

Sebire H.R. 1985 A Roman Samian Mortarium *Trans. Soc. Guernesiaise* Vol XXI, pp 720-722

Sinel, J. 1914 *Prehistoric Times and the Men of the Channel Islands,* Jersey.

Stevens-Cox, J. 1976 *Prehistoric Monuments of Guernsey and Associated Folklore.* Toucan Press St Peter Port.

Winterflood A. 1956 Menhir at Le Crocq, St Saviour. *Trans. Soc. Guernesiaise* Vol XVI p 16.

Notes on the Contributors

Kenneth J. Barton

Ken Barton is the former Director of Hampshire County Museum Service. He has excavated extensively in the Channel Islands but particularly in Guernsey where he examined the medieval and later fortifications. He is currently writing the report on the series of excavations at Castle Cornet, Guernsey which is eagerly awaited. He is now retired and living in Normandy.

Michael Batt

Michael Batt is an archaeology graduate from Cardiff University but for many years has been working for the French Government Archaeology Service in Rennes. He has visited Guernsey many times and has been particularly helpful in drawing Breton parallels with our Channel Island sites. He lives in Rennes with his French wife and family.

Michael Bowyer

Michael Bowyer has been involved in diving projects for many years while running an engineering business. He graduated in Marine Archaeology from Bangor University in 1992. Since that time he has been Director of Marine Archaeology Studies at Bangor and has been involved with many marine sites in Wales such as the Bronze Bell in Cardigan Bay. He was Site Director of the Alderney project from 1993-1996.

Duncan Brown

Duncan Brown is Keeper of Finds at Southampton City Museums. He has published many papers on medieval pottery and is Secretary of the Medieval Pottery Research Group. In partnership with Bob Thomson he has studied the medieval pottery of Guernsey and is currently engaged on a project studying medieval pottery from St Peter Port Harbour.

Nicky David

Nicky David has since the late 1970s studied the clay pipes from excavations in Guernsey. She has attended conferences and published various papers on clay pipes. A major piece of work that she has undertaken recently is the report on the huge assemblage of pipes from Castle Cornet, Guernsey.

Vivien Ferneyhough

Vivien Ferneyhough has recently begun to study glass in Guernsey with a particular interest in the glass from excavations. She has a degree in Fine Arts and has become expert in her field in a relatively short time due to the considerable commitment she has made in time and effort. With her husband she runs a local jewellery business.

Margaret Finlaison

Margaret Finlaison has since the 1970s been the mainstay of archaeology in Jersey. She is a former Chairman of the Archaeological Section of Société Jersiaise and a member of the States of Jersey Historic Monuments Advisory Committee. She has excavated extensively in Jersey particularly around St Helier and is currently writing reports on various sites which she has excavated.

Pierre-Roland Giot

Pierre-Roland Giot was formerly Head of the Laboratoire d'Anthropologie at Rennes University. He has published widely on all aspects of prehistory of Britanny and has always taken an interest in Guernsey archaeology and our Breton connections.

Katherine Gruel

Katherine Gruel now works for the French Government Archaeology Service in Paris. She has particularly studied the Iron Age coinage of the Coriosolites tribe and has included the Jersey hoards in her studies.

Mike Hill

Mike Hill until recently lived in Guernsey and was an extraordinary field worker. He single handedly explored the cliffs and coast line of Guernsey and collated a great deal of information about sites , many of which were hitherto unrecorded.

Richard Hocart

Richard Hocart is a historian who lives and works in his native Guernsey. He has published widely on local history subjects and in particular a scholarly work on the local parliament the States of Guernsey, entitled "An Island Assembly".

Philip de Jersey

Philip de Jersey is a Research Assistant at the Institute of Archaeology in Oxford maintaining the register of Celtic Coinage. He was born and grew up in Guernsey and has dug on many local sites since the mid 1980s. His doctoral thesis at Oxford was on the Celtic Coinage of Armorica.

Ian Kinnes

Ian Kinnes is an Assistant Keeper in the department of Prehistoric and Romano-British Antiquities at the British Museum. He excavated the site of Les Fouaillages in Guernsey, a newly discovered burial tomb, in the early 1980s and has been supportive of the study of the earliest phases of occupation in Guernsey ever since.

Jason Monaghan

Jason Monaghan is a Roman pottery specialist who worked for several years for the York Archaeological Trust. He now lives in Guernsey and worked on and jointly published with Margaret Rule, the report on the Gallo-Roman trading vessel that was found in St Peter Port harbour. He continues to do freelance archaeology projects.

Darryl Ogier

Darryl Ogier is a History graduate from Warwick University who chose Society in Guernsey c.1500-1640 as the subject of his doctoral research. He lives in the island and has recently been appointed Island Archivist to the States of Guernsey.

Bob Thomson

Until his retirement Bob Thomson was Keeper of Archaeology in Southampton. He visited Guernsey many times during Kenneth Barton's excavations to study the pottery from the Channel Islands. He is now a pottery consultant and is currently working on a cargo of medieval pottery from a shipwreck in St Peter Port harbour.

Heather Sebire

Heather Sebire worked in archaeology in London, after graduating, for Southwark Excavation Committee and later the Inner London Unit. She then was Archaeological Liaison Officer for British Gas on their Southern Feeder pipeline. After going to live in Guernsey she became secretary of the Archaeology Section of La Société Guernesiaise and as such has been actively involved in local archaeology over the last fifteen years. After Bob Burns retirement in 1995, she was appointed Archaeology Officer at Guernsey Museum.